KEYS TO NUTRITION OVER FIFTY

Jo Murphy
Gerontologist

BARRON'S

All inquiries should be addressed to:
Barron's Educational Series, Inc.
250 Wireless Boulevard
Hauppauge, New York 11788

Library of Congress Catalog Card No. 91-21093
International Standard Book No. 0-8120-4512-2

Library of Congress Cataloging-in-Publication Data
Murphy, Jo.
    Keys to nutrition over fifty / by Jo Murphy.
        p. cm.
    Includes index.
    ISBN 0-8120-4512-2
    1. Aged—Nutrition.   I. Title.
RA777.6.M37   1991
613.2'084'6—dc20

91-21093
CIP

PRINTED IN THE UNITED STATES OF AMERICA

1234   5500   987654321

Dedication

To my husband Bill who has progressed with me through book number two. Thank you for your love, devotion, and friendship. Good luck with fitness and nutrition.

CONTENTS

ACKNOWLEDGMENTS

I could not have made the "deadline" without the support of my sister and friend, Betty Sims. She assisted me in editing and correcting my first book, *Keys to Fitness Over Fifty,* and did another marvelous job of refining *Keys to Nutrition Over Fifty.*

I would also like to credit the following federal, state and local government agencies, whose bulletins, booklets, brochures, and videos simplified my job: the Department of Health and Human Services, the Department of Agriculture, the Food and Drug Administration, the Environmental Protection Agency, Colorado State University Cooperative Extension, the Colorado Department of Food Science and Human Nutrition and Tri-County Health in Englewood, Colorado.

Thank you to Connie Auran, M.S., R.D., for her conscientious effort to help with the formulation of the 50 keys in this book and for her review of the manuscript.

My appreciation to Tamara Nelson, M.S., R.D., who specializes in geriatric nutrition. She verified the accuracy of the material, developed the charts, and compiled questions common to geriatric nutrition.

My gratitude to Barron's Educational Series, Inc. for allowing me to write a second book in the retirement series. And to my editor Carolyn Horne, for her patience and professional expertise.

And most important, to you, the readers of this book, who are willing to grow, learn, change, and improve the quality of your life.

INTRODUCTION

Welcome to the wonderful, challenging, ever changing, and sometimes confusing world of nutrition over age fifty. Nutrition should be considered carefully as we grow older. It is a major key to maintaining an excellent quality of life as we age.

It will be impossible to go into detail in every Key, but I hope to cover, as the song says, "a little bit about a lot of things." Intelligent changes in your nutrition habits will result in a more productive, positive, and energetic life.

The study of nutrition is not an exact science, but each decade of research helps us uncover the needs of our bodies. There is no universal formula that works for everyone. As in all areas of health, every individual is different and must be treated as such. There are many variables to consider.

In my many years of teaching nutrition to senior citizen classes, I have come to realize that the main factor is changing attitude. If you are willing to keep all the doors open, learn new ideas, and put them into practice, your quality of life can be enhanced.

None of the concepts, suggestions, information, and ideas in this book are meant to replace proper professional diagnosis, treatment, or help. If you have nutrition and health concerns, always seek proper professional guidance.

Many months have been spent verifying all statements, research, studies, and references for accuracy. In nutrition, like all fields, varied opinions create controversy. With further research new dimensions will be added to the field of nutrition.

My aim in this book is to inform, motivate, and inspire you to consider making any necessary changes relating to your nutritional needs. It can affect many areas of your life.

1

TOTAL FITNESS

The popularity of fitness is growing by leaps and bounds. Is there such a thing as total or complete fitness? Although there is no cure for "old age," you can improve your fitness level to enhance your daily activities. In this sense, total fitness is having the physical stamina to carry out whatever it is you personally aspire to do. With life expectancy increasing year after year, it is a necessity to get on the bandwagon and maintain your quality of life as the years progress.

If you read my first book, *Keys to Fitness Over Fifty*, you know the importance of all aspects of health. It is my opinion that there are four broad areas of fitness: physical, mental, emotional, and spiritual. We covered all of those areas in detail in that book and it is important to understand the interconnection. How do these four areas fit into the master plan and pertain to nutrition?

Approaching nutrition physically, mentally, emotionally, and spiritually is intriguing to me. But, if you contemplate it, it makes sense. The physical aspects of nutrition extend from shopping, to preparing and cooking the food, to eating. Mentally we think about food a lot; it is a big part of our lives. Also we must have the mental capabilities to understand nutrition and to read grocery ads, recipes, and so on. Food and eating are very emotional issues. In fact, many people believe this is the strongest urge; many people use food to fulfill an emotional need. The connection between spirituality and food dates back to before biblical times. Many examples of the spiritual aspect of food can be cited in the Bible. Look at the culture and inheritance of all nationalities and you can see a great spiritual need being met with food. While you absorb the information in the following Keys, keep in mind the four aspects of fitness.

Let's move on to another total fitness concept, lifestyle. Lifestyle can be defined in many ways, but simply put, it is all of your accumulated behaviors and habits and how you live on a day-to-day basis. To be totally fit and maintain optimal health, we must strive for the best lifestyle possible. This takes time, energy, commitment, and perseverance. Reading this book and following good nutrition habits will not guarantee longevity and quality of life if other areas of our lives are unhealthy.

Good health depends on a combination of things besides personal behavior and habits. Heredity plays an important role, and so does the environment you live in, the medical care you receive, and most important, your outlook on life.

The U.S. Department of Health and Human Services has developed a wonderful Healthstyle test that I would like to encourage you to take. This test actually may add years to your life! It will enable you to identify aspects of your present lifestyle that are risky to your health and point out where you need to make changes. It also will help you feel good about yourself in the areas where you already are doing an admirable job.

The test has six sections: smoking, alcohol and drugs, eating habits, exercise and fitness, stress control, and safety. Complete one section at a time by circling the number corresponding to the answer that best describes your behavior (2 for "Almost Always," 1 for "Sometimes," and 0 for "Almost Never"). Then add the numbers you have circled to determine your score for that section. The highest score you can get for each section is 10.

This is not a passfail test. It also is not meant for any particular age group. Its purpose simply is to tell you how well you are doing in maintaining good health. Good luck!

After you have completed the test, read what your score means and what you can to do reduce your risk of disease and premature death and to enjoy a healthier lifestyle.

In 1990, the U.S. Department of Health and Human Services announced Healthy People 2000, a set of national health goals, which include eating well, exercising, and practicing lifestyle habits to keep you and your family healthier longer. Also, A.A.R.P. (American Association of Retired Persons) plans to participate in this campaign by focusing on health issues of special significance to persons over age fifty.

With the life expectancy increasing dramatically and health care costs rising sharply, each one of us must make a commitment to strive for total fitness.

A Test for Better Health

	Almost Always	Sometimes	Almost Never
If you never smoke, enter a score of 10 for this section and go to the next section on *Alcohol and Drugs*.			
1. I avoid smoking cigarettes.	2	1	0
2. I smoke only low tar and nicotine cigarettes *or* I smoke a pipe or cigars.	2	1	0

Smoking Score: _____

	Almost Always	Sometimes	Almost Never
1. I avoid drinking alcoholic beverages *or* I drink no more than 1 or 2 drinks a day.	4	1	0
2. I avoid using alcohol or other drugs (especially illegal drugs) as a way of handling stressful situations or the problems in my life.	2	1	0
3. I am careful not to drink alcohol when taking certain medicines (for example, medicine for sleeping, pain, colds, and allergies).	2	1	0

	Almost Always	Sometimes	Almost Never
4. I read and follow the label directions when using prescribed and over-the-counter drugs.	2	1	0

Alcohol and Drugs Score: _____

Eating Habits

	Almost Always	Sometimes	Almost Never
1. I eat a variety of foods each day, such as fruits and vegetables, whole grain breads and cereals, lean meats, dairy products, dry peas and beans, and nuts and seeds.	4	1	0
2. I limit the amount of fat, saturated fat, and cholesterol I eat (including fat on meats, eggs, butter, cream, shortenings, and organ meats such as liver).	2	1	0
3. I limit the amount of salt I eat by cooking with only small amounts, not adding salt at the table, and avoiding salty snacks.	2	1	0
4. I avoid eating too much sugar (especially frequent snacks of sticky candy or soft drinks).	2	1	0

Eating Habits Score: _____

Exercise/Fitness

	Almost Always	Sometimes	Almost Never
1. I maintain a desired weight, avoiding overweight and underweight.	3	1	0

	Almost Always	Sometimes	Almost Never
2. I do vigorous exercises for 15–30 minutes at least 3 times a week (examples include running, swimming, brisk walking).	3	1	0
3. I do exercises that enhance my muscle tone for 15–30 minutes at least 3 times a week (examples include yoga and calisthenics)	2	1	0
4. I use part of my leisure time participating in individual, family, or team activities that increase my level of fitness (such as gardening, bowling, golf, and baseball).	2	1	0

Exercise/Fitness Score: _____

Stress Control

1. I have a job or do other work that I enjoy.	2	1	0
2. I find it easy to relax and express my feelings freely.	2	1	0
3. I recognize early and prepare for events or situations likely to be stressful for me.	2	1	0
4. I have close friends, relatives, or others whom I can talk to about personal matters and call on for help when needed	2	1	0
5. I participate in group activities (such as church and community organizations) or hobbies that I enjoy.	2	1	0

Stress Control Score: _____

Safety

	Almost Always	Sometimes	Almost Never
1. I wear a seat belt while riding in a car.	2	1	0
2. I avoid driving while under the influence of alcohol and other drugs.	2	1	0
3. I obey traffic rules and the speed limit when driving.	2	1	0
4. I am careful when using potentially harmful products or substances (such as household cleaners, poisons, and electrical devices).	2	1	0
5. I avoid smoking in bed.	2	1	0

Safety Score: _____

Your HEALTHSTYLE Scores

After you have figured your scores for each of the six sections, circle the number in each column that matches your score for that section of the test.

Cigarette Smoking	Alcohol and Drugs	Eating Habits	Exercise/ Fitness	Stress Control	Safety
10	10	10	10	10	10
9	9	9	9	9	9
8	8	8	8	8	8
7	7	7	7	7	7
6	6	6	6	6	6
5	5	5	5	5	5
4	4	4	4	4	4
3	3	3	3	3	3
2	2	2	2	2	2
1	1	1	1	1	1
0	0	0	0	0	0

Remember, there is no total score for this test. Consider each section separately. You are trying to identify aspects of your lifestyle that you can improve in order to be healthier and to reduce the risk of illness. So let's see what your scores reveal.

What Your Scores Mean to YOU

Scores of 9 and 10

Excellent! Your answers show that you are aware of the importance of this area to your health. More importantly, you are putting your knowledge to work for you by practicing good health habits. As long as you continue to do so, this area should not pose a serious health risk. It's likely that you are setting an example for your family and friends to follow. Since you got a very high score on this part of the test, you may want to consider other areas where your scores indicate room for improvement.

Scores of 6–8

Your health practices in this area are good, but there is room for improvement. Look again at the items you answered with a "Sometimes" or "Almost Never." What changes can you make to improve your score? Even a small change can often help you achieve better health.

Scores of 3–5

Your health risks are showing! Would you like more information about the risks you are facing and about why it is important for you to change these behaviors? Perhaps you need help in deciding how to successfully make the changes you desire. In either case, help is available. See the last page of this test.

Scores of 0–2

Obviously, you were concerned enough about your health to take the test, but your answers show that you may be taking serious and unnecessary risks with your health. Perhaps you are not aware of the risks and what to do about them. You can easily get the information and help you need to improve, if you wish. The next step is up to you.

YOU Can Start Right Now!

In the test you just completed were numerous suggestions to help you reduce your risk of disease and premature death. Here are some of the most significant:

Avoid cigarettes. Cigarette smoking is the single most important preventable cause of illness and early death. It is especially risky for pregnant women and their unborn babies. Persons who stop smoking reduce their risk of getting heart disease and cancer. So if you're a cigarette smoker, think twice about lighting that next cigarette. If you choose to continue smoking, try decreasing the number of cigarettes you smoke and switching to a low tar and nicotine brand.

Follow sensible drinking habits. Alcohol produces changes in mood and behavior. Most people who drink are able to control their intake of alcohol and to avoid undesired, and often harmful, effects. Heavy, regular use of alcohol can lead to cirrhosis of the liver, a leading cause of death. Also, statistics clearly show that mixing drinking and driving is often the cause of fatal or crippling accidents. So if you drink, do it wisely and in moderation.

Use care in taking drugs. Today's greater use of drugs—both legal and illegal—is one of our most serious health risks. Even some drugs prescribed by your doctor can be dangerous if taken when drinking alcohol or before driving. Excessive or continued use of tranquilizers (or "pep pills") can cause physical and mental problems. Using or experimenting with illicit drugs such as marijuana, heroin, cocaine, and PCP may lead to a number of damaging effects or even death.

Eat sensibly. Overweight individuals are at greater risk for diabetes, gallbladder disease, and high blood pressure. So it makes good sense to maintain proper weight. But good eating habits also mean holding down the amount of fat (especially

9

saturated fat), cholesterol, sugar, and salt in your diet. If you must snack, try nibbling on fresh fruits and vegetables. You'll feel better—and look better too.

Exercise regularly. Almost everyone can benefit from exercise—and there's some form of exercise almost everyone can do. (If you have any doubt, check first with your doctor.) Usually, as little as 15–30 minutes of vigorous exercise three times a week will help you have a healthier heart, eliminate excess weight, tone up sagging muscles, and sleep better. Think how much difference all these improvements could make in the way you feel!

Learn to handle stress. Stress is a normal part of living; everyone faces it to some degree. The causes of stress can be good or bad, desirable or undesirable (such as a promotion on the job or the loss of a spouse). Properly handled, stress need not be a problem. But unhealthy responses to stress—such as driving too fast or erratically, drinking too much, or prolonged anger or grief—can cause a variety of physical and mental problems. Even on a very busy day, find a few minutes to slow down and relax. Talking over a problem with someone you trust can often help you find a satisfactory solution. Learn to distinguish between things that are "worth fighting about" and things that are less important.

Be safety conscious. Think "safety first" at home, at work, at school, at play, and on the highway. Buckle seat belts and obey traffic rules. Keep poisons and weapons out of the reach of children, and keep emergency numbers by your telephone. When the unexpected happens, you'll be prepared.

Where Do You Go From Here?

Start by asking yourself a few frank questions:
Am I really doing all I can to be as healthy as possible? What steps can I take to feel better? Am I willing to begin now? If you scored low in one or more sections of the test, decide what changes you want to make for improvement. You might

pick that aspect of your lifestyle where you feel you have the best chance for success and tackle that one first. Once you have improved your score there, go on to other areas.

If you already have tried to change your health habits (to stop smoking or exercise regularly, for example) don't be discouraged if you haven't yet succeeded. The difficulty you have encountered may be due to influences you've never really thought about—such as advertising—or to a lack of support and encouragement. Understanding these influences is an important step toward changing the way they affect you.

There's Help Available. In addition to personal actions you can take on your own, there are community programs and groups (such as the YMCA or the local chapter of the American Heart Association) that can assist you and your family to make the changes you want to make. If you want to know more about these groups or about health risks, contact your local health department. There's a lot you can do to stay healthy or to improve your health—and there are organizations that can help you. Start a new HEALTHSTYLE today!

2

TOTAL NUTRITION

Is there such a thing as complete and totally adequate nutrition? Ideal nutrition does not exist, but we know for optimal health and fitness we all must strive for the best eating habits possible. This requires dedication, knowledge, perseverance, and the ability to constantly grow and change.

Nutrients are chemical substances obtained from foods during digestion. They are needed to build and maintain body cells, regulate body processes, and supply energy. There are over 40 nutrients considered essential for health. We get these nutrients from six sources: water, protein, carbohydrate, fat, vitamins, and minerals. There is a fine balance to be maintained to make sure we are getting sufficient nutrition in all of these areas. Because of the complications that go along with the aging process, it is imperative that we spend more time eating right. Many older people believe they are eating a balanced diet, when in fact signs of malnutrition can go undetected.

Our body can be compared to a furnace. The calories we put into it are like fuel. The body needs the fuel to supply energy for all of our bodily processes such as breathing, blood circulation, digestion, and exercise. As we get older, the amount of body fat increases and lean muscle decreases. Meanwhile, the need for vitamins and minerals remains the same and even increases in many cases. The National Research Council recommends a reduction in calorie intake for both men and women after age fifty. Seniors need to be especially mindful of food choices, avoiding foods high in fat and calories such as sweets, pastries, cakes, and cookies. Scientists are still in the process of researching what nutrients are necessary for different age groups. They agree that a distinct differentiation is needed between requirements for fifty-year olds and each following decade. In the Keys that follow, we will be discussing these important nutrients in detail.

There are general guidelines that make up total nutrition: In 1990, the U.S. Department of Agriculture and Health and Human Services had some updated advice. On the following page is a chart of the seven guidelines.

Understanding the food groups and the amounts necessary for daily minimum consumption is very important. The four food groups concept is a marvelous design; if you select from the four food groups on a daily basis, you are quite likely to meet all your nutrient needs. Please try to memorize the convenient food chart that follows. When studying the chart, keep in mind that the need for calcium increases with age. It may be beneficial to increase dairy-rich foods to three to four servings each day. These dairy foods also are present in protein and may count as a meat serving. For instance, a cheese sandwich for lunch could replace a peanut butter or turkey sandwich, and still count as one of your meat servings.

If you want to remain productive and active in later life, it is imperative that you heed the basic minimum requirements. The physiological changes that occur as we age take place very gradually. Many problems can be attributed to genetic traits, illnesses, life events, and how well we ate during the earlier years of our life. Dietary habits that have been developed over a lifetime are a prime consideration. It is a challenge to obtain adequate supplies of all nutrients while reducing calories.

Make it your goal to strive for the best nutrition possible!

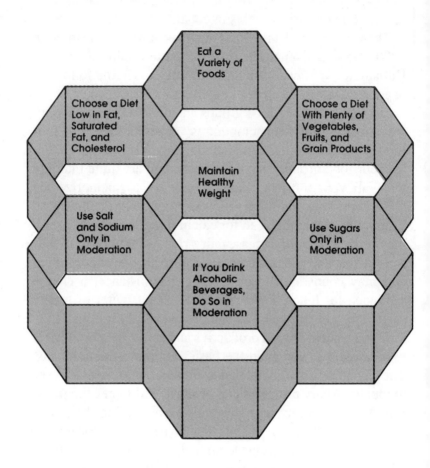

**Use the seven guidelines together
as you choose a healthful and enjoyable diet.**

Four Food Groups

Food Group	Number of Servings per day	Serving Size	Major Nutrients
Dairy	2–3	1 cup milk 1 cup yogurt 1 oz. cheese $\frac{1}{2}$ cup cottage cheese $\frac{1}{2}$ cup ice cream, ice milk, or frozen yogurt	protein fat carbohydrate calcium riboflavin
Meat	2	2–3 oz. cooked lean beef, pork, lamb, fish, or poultry 1 egg $\frac{1}{2}$ cup cooked dried peas or beans/legumes 2 tbsp. peanut butter $\frac{1}{4}$ cup nuts or seeds	protein fat iron thiamin niacin
Fruit, Vegetable	3–5	$\frac{1}{2}$ cup juice $\frac{1}{2}$ cup cooked vegetable 1 cup raw vegetable $\frac{1}{2}$ cup fruit 1 medium apple, banana, orange, or peach $\frac{1}{2}$ grapefruit $\frac{1}{3}$ cantaloupe $\frac{1}{4}$ cup dried fruit	carbohydrate vitamin A vitamin C fiber
Grain	6–11	1 slice bread $\frac{1}{2}$ English muffin or hamburger bun 1 oz. ready-to-eat cereal $\frac{1}{2}$ cup pasta, cooked cereal, grits, or mashed potatoes $\frac{1}{3}$ cup rice 1 medium potato 1 tortilla, roll, or muffin	carbohydrate protein thiamin niacin iron fiber

3

THE FIVE SENSES

The five senses are important to all aspects of life. We were born with them and tend to take them for granted. All the five senses are very important when it comes to nutrition. Let us explore the different ways taste, smell, sight, touch, and hearing are involved with nutrition.

Taste: Taste is influenced by all the other senses: smell or aroma, the sight or form and color of food, the feel or texture, and even the sounds it makes as it cooks. The first sense we automatically think of is taste. It probably is the most influential and important aspect of enjoying food. There are really only four different kinds of taste—sweet, sour, salty, and bitter. The combination of these produce all the range of food pleasures we have come to know.

As we age, there can be a change in our ability to taste due to a reduced sensitivity and number of taste buds. This can be a result of chronic disease and the use of multiple medications and lead to a disinterest in food and proper nutrition. We can oversalt things and use too many hot spices to try to get the taste back, when in fact what we are doing is masking the true taste.

Food cravings can be attributed to taste and can lead to an unbalanced diet. We all probably have had the experience of the immense desire for something sweet, like chocolate, or something salty, like peanuts. The sour and bitter usually are less of a craving, but also can become a problem.

Smell: My favorite list of smells and aromas is very long, going way back to my childhood: The smell of freshly baked bread when I came home from school. The holidays when I could smell the turkey roasting and pies baking. The smell of coffee, onions, spices, and herbs. The sense of smell also can be negative and a warning sign, perhaps of something burning.

One of my weaknesses has always been to boil potatoes and let the water evaporate. Oh dear! Other negative smells are burning toast, oven spills, and so on. The sense of smell diminishes gradually as we age, but it can be a sign of a more serious medical problem.

Sight: If you notice all of the food commercials on television, you know the power and influence of sight on your eating habits. They really tempt your willpower and make it very hard to resist even the food that you know is not good for you. At the grocery store, foods are packaged and displayed using bright, attention-getting colors. At the University of Massachusetts Food Science Department, they have been studying how color affects our perception of sweetness. Red turned out to be the most powerful influence, and anything red appeared sweeter. Perhaps more emphasis should be placed on making a colorful attractive plate to spark healthier eating.

As our sight diminishes, it also becomes a problem to read recipes, newspaper ads, prices, and food labels. Our interest in planning meals, shopping, and cooking can lessen. A real fear of cooking can develop. Even dining out is not a pleasure if we cannot read the menu.

Touch: The texture of food—soft, hard, fibrous, smooth, liquid, solid—plays a major role in nutrition. I know a man who rejects smooth pudding because when he grew up his mother always made it lumpy. Before utensils were invented, people ate with their fingers, so the sense of touch was more important then. If you cannot see or hear, the sense of touch takes on more importance. Many times poor circulation will interfere with our sense of touch and the feel of food, cooking surfaces, and utensils is inaccurate. The sense of touch is important to tell hot from cold and can be vital so that we do not burn ourselves.

Hearing: What do you hear on your nutrition list? Perhaps popcorn popping, carrots and celery crunching, chicken frying (not any more), coffee perking, vegetables boiling, the snap, crackle, and pop of cereal, and the sizzle of barbecuing and broiling. Perhaps hearing is an aspect of nutrition you did not think about.

Remember the negative—if you cannot hear, you might not want to go out to a restaurant or be around other people. Perhaps you do not want to go grocery shopping because it is too confusing.

The five senses are an extremely powerful influence on all aspects of nutrition. They are very positive forces and we need to be aware when the positive turns to a negative and we need to seek medical attention for our taste, smell, sight, touch, or hearing.

It is important to keep all of the five senses in mind when reading and implementing the other Keys in this book.

4

LET'S GO SHOPPING

When we hear someone saying, "Let's go shopping," each one of us conjures up different memories of grocery shopping, from dreaded experiences to warm, friendly thoughts. Perhaps you remember shopping as a child with your mother. Can you remember going to the meat market, bakery, creamery, farmer's market, and grocery store? Quite a project! In many countries, shopping for food still is done that way. Growing up on a farm was even a different experience. We had a huge garden for all of our own produce, cows for milk and cream, and access to beef, pork, lamb, and poultry. It was a real treat to go to town to the grocery store. What a difference between that experience and the one-stop supermarket that we know of today. Grocery shopping can be a negative or a positive adventure, and is the topic for many of the following Keys. It is where good nutrition starts, no matter what age group you are in.

Menu Planning: The secret to successful shopping is to plan ahead. Menu planning can be a real art and is the basis for smart shopping. With age and possibly short-term memory, it is even more critical to take time to think out your eating plans. To plan your shopping list, divide a sheet of paper into four boxes; each box represents one of the four food groups. Then make out your list. Have your weekly schedule in front of you so you know what days you will be away from home, when you have outside activities, perhaps when you want to entertain, and what social and work commitments you have. Do you have a different schedule on weekends than during the week?

Remember, careful planning also can help you cut down on impulse buying at the store, help you avoid waste, and save you time for other activities. Often the perimeter of the store has all the food you need. The meat, dairy, bread/grain, and fruits and

Shopping List

Meat	Dairy
~~	~~~~~~
~~	~~~~~~
~~	~~~~~
	~~

Bread	Fruit
~~	~~~~~~~
~~	~~~~~
~~	
~~	Vegetable

Condiments
~~~~~~ ~~~~~~
~~~~~~~

Household items
~~~~~~ ~~~~~~   ~~~~
~~~~~~~ ~~~~

vegetables are all on the sides. You can get yourself into trouble when you venture into the center sections.

What is your meal pattern? A large nutritious breakfast or a small and simple one? Perhaps you are at the stage of life where your main meal is at noon and you have a lighter meal at night. Do you prepare all of your food from scratch or use a lot of convenience foods? Are you shopping and cooking for one or two people? Do you or does someone in your family have dietary needs or health problems that require a special diet? Menu planning is very individual and every concern should be addressed. Of course, all of us have been planning menus, shopping, and cooking for years, but we always can learn something new. It is possible to get out of our rut and put some fun and enthusiasm back into something we have been doing forever.

What else is important when planning meals besides making sure you have a well-balanced, nutritious diet? Variety also is important when thinking about different textures, colors, flavors, and ways to prepare food. Consider seasonal foods and the seasons of the year, like foods suitably warm in winter and cool for summer. Have your old favorites, but introduce new food and recipes too.

Writing down your food intake for breakfast, lunch, and dinner, and morning, afternoon, and evening snacks is a good way to determine whether you are getting all the necessary nutrients each day. If you find that you consistently are omitting any given food group, then you are denying yourself the nutrients abundant in that food group. Keep a list of the staples you have in your pantry, refrigerator, and freezer.

Budget: No matter what your age, it is a real challenge to be able to get your "money's worth" at the supermarket. Budget plans usually are categorized into thrifty, low-cost, moderate, and liberal. Costs depend on many factors: where you buy your food, how carefully you plan, how much prepared or convenience food is used, how many people are in your family, and so on.

Take advantage of the weekly advertised specials, coupons, and the variety of generic products available. By all means, if you are eligible for food stamps, use them. Comparing prices takes time but really can help the food budget. Many supermarkets provide a quick and easy way to compare prices. It's called *unit pricing*. The unit price label shows both the retail price and the price per pound, ounce, quart, or other unit. Comparing the unit price among brands and container sizes of a product can help you find the best buys. Unit pricing information usually is located on the shelf edge, directly below or above the item.

Open dating can help you select the freshest products in the supermarket. There are four basic types of open dates on food labels. *Pull by or sell by* date is used on foods such as dairy products and packaged meats. The pull by date means it allows you enough time to use the product at home. Expiration or *use by* date can be found on refrigerated doughs and eggs. *Pack date* is the date the food was manufactured, processed and packaged. This usually is done for canned goods. Freshness or *best-if-used-by* date is used on products such as bakery goods or packaged cereals. It pays to check these dates. If you do not understand a code, have a grocery clerk or store manager explain it to you. Store personnel are there for you.

We now have some general guidelines for shopping. Get your coat on; don't forget your grocery list and checkbook, and let's go shopping!

5

LABEL READING

It is imperative that we understand and read the labels of the food we are purchasing at the supermarket. We don't need a calorie counter, calculator, and magnifying glass in hand when we go to the grocery store. I will try and simplify some of the label reading that is now on the products we purchase. Hopefully at this writing, the government and manufacturers are now making progress in standardizing, clarifying, and changing many of the labeling laws.

Why is it important as we grow older to take the time to read labels when we grocery shop? More and more age fifty-plus people are concerned about their fat and cholesterol consumption, salt intake, fiber content, and weight control. The labels on all products should give this information clearly and without confusion. We also need to compare products and avoid being misled by them.

Congress, the FDA (Food and Drug Administration), the USDA (U.S. Department of Agriculture), other government agencies, health organizations, consumer groups, and the food industry are all diligently working at easing the burden of complicated food labeling and simplifying it.

The USRDA (U.S. Recommended Daily Allowances) were developed for use in nutrition labeling of food products. Remember, nutrient needs vary among individuals and they are set high to cover the needs of a wide spectrum of the population. A typical food label today has on it the following information: percentages of the RDA of protein, five vitamins, and two minerals in a serving; serving size, number of servings per container; and calories, protein, carbohydrate, fat, and sodium per serving of the product. Each can vary but most manufacturers are listing more and more information for the benefit of consumers.

The FDA requires all packaged foods to carry a label that gives the name of the product, name and location of the manufacturer, packer, or distributor, and the net content and weight. Labels also must list ingredients by specific name, in descending order of weight. Health claims have gotten out of control and need evaluating. However, some claims have been substantiated scientifically, including calcium and a lower risk of osteoporosis, a low-fat diet and cancer, a low-fat diet and heart disease, a low-salt diet and hypertension, fiber and cancer, and fiber and cardiovascular disease.

One of the best ways to be confident that you are making the right food choice is to know some of the definitions commonly used on labels and how misleading some of them are. One time my husband and I bought a bag of corn chips that claimed to be "lite." I thought it meant low-fat and therefore low in calories. Bill thought it was low in sodium. It turned out that the chips were made from white corn and thus "lite" in color! Just one example of confusion when reading labels.

The FDA and USDA set labeling criteria. Some of the general FDA criteria in regard to calories are as follows:

Diet, dietetic: Must be described clearly as useful for a special dietary purpose and must meet the same requirements for low calorie or reduced calorie. The USDA also has labeling criteria.

Lite: There really is no set definition for the term lite (or light). One definition is significantly fewer calories, less fat, and at least 25 percent less salt than the original product.

Low calorie: No more than 40 calories per serving. A food that is naturally low in calories cannot carry this label.

Reduced calorie: The food is at least one-third lower than that of the food to which it is being compared.

The USDA defines sodium claims as follows:

Low sodium: No more than 140 milligrams sodium per serving.

Reduced sodium: Processed to reduce the usual sodium level by 75 percent. The label must compare the product's sodium content to that of the food being replaced.

Salt-free, no salt added, unsalted: Products that are processed without salt. But they still can contain sodium naturally.

Sodium-free: Less than 5 milligrams sodium per serving.

Very low sodium: No more than 35 milligrams sodium per serving.

The USDA defines these terms in regard to meats and poultry, except for ground beef and hamburger.

Lean, low fat: No more than 10 percent fat by weight.

Extra lean: No more than 5 percent fat by weight.

Lite, light, leaner: At least 25 percent less fat than the original product.

Reduced cholesterol: At least a 75 percent reduction as compared to a similar food.

Hopefully this will give you some insight into the importance of understanding how to read labels. Almost all the grocery shopping and healthy heart classes teach you the proper way to read labels. I encourage you to take one of these classes. At this very writing reforms and legislation are under way to change labels and clear up some of the confusion for consumers.

MIXED VEGETABLES

NUTRITION INFORMATION PER SERVING

SERVING SIZE: ½ CUP

SERVINGS PER CONTAINER: 4

CALORIES 45	FAT 0g
PROTEIN 1g	SODIUM 390mg
CARBOHYDRATE 7g	

PERCENTAGE OF U.S. RECOMMENDED DAILY ALLOWANCES (U.S. RDA)

PROTEIN 2	RIBOFLAVIN 2
VITAMIN A 90	NIACIN 2
VITAMIN C 8	CALCIUM 2
THIAMINE 2	IRON..2

INGREDIENTS: WATER, CARROTS, WHITE POTATOES, CELERY, SWEET PEAS, GREEN BEANS, GOLDEN CORN, LIMA BEANS, SALT, ONION POWDER, CALCIUM CHLORIDE ADDED AS A FIRMING AGENT.

DIST. BY VALU TIME DIVISION, TOPCO ASSOC., INC., SKOKIE, IL 60076

NET WT   453 GRAMS   WT OF MIXED

VEGETABLES** ....276 GRAMS

**WEIGHT OF MIXED VEGETABLES MEANS WEIGHT BEFORE ADDITION OF LIQUID NECESSARY FOR PROCESSING.

HOW TO READ A FOOD LABEL

Serving size and number of servings per container must be listed. When comparing brands, make sure serving sizes are the same.

This part of the label tells the number of calories and the amount of protein, carbohydrate, fat, and sodium present in one serving of the product.

Listing of these eight nutrients is required.

Others are optional unless they have been added or a nutritional claim is made for them.

Ingredients must be identified by their common names. The ingredient present in the largest amount by weight must be listed first, followed by other ingredients in descending order.

BREAKFAST CEREAL
All Natural

NUTRITION INFORMATION PER SERVING

SERVING SIZE: 1 OZ.
(ABOUT ⅞ CUP) (28.35 g)
SERVINGS PER PACKAGE: 12

	1 OZ. CEREAL	WITH ½ CUP VITAMIN D FORTIFIED WHOLE MILK
CALORIES	100	180 *
PROTEIN	3 g	7 g
CARBOHYDRATE	23 g	29 g
FAT	1 g	5 g
SODIUM	160 mg	220 mg

PERCENTAGES OF U.S. RECOMMENDED DAILY ALLOWANCES (U.S. RDA)

PROTEIN	4%	10%
VITAMIN A	25%	30%
VITAMIN C	**	**
THIAMINE	25%	30%
RIBOFLAVIN	25%	35%
NIACIN	25%	25%
CALCIUM	**	15%
IRON	45%	45%
VITAMIN D	10%	25%
VITAMIN B_6	25%	30%
FOLIC ACID	25%	25%
VITAMIN B_{12}	25%	30%
PHOSPHORUS	8%	20%
MAGNESIUM	8%	10%
ZINC	8%	10%
COPPER	6%	6%

* SAVE 30 CALORIES—USE SKIM MILK.
** CONTAINS LESS THAN 2% OF THE U.S. RDA OF THESE NUTRIENTS.

INGREDIENTS: NATURAL WHOLE WHEAT, MALTED BARLEY, SUGAR, COCONUT OIL AND SALT.

VITAMINS & MINERALS: IRON, VITAMIN A PALMITATE, NIACINAMIDE, ZINC OXIDE (SOURCE OF ZINC), VITAMIN B RIBOFLAVIN (VITAMIN B_2). THIAMINE MONONITRATE (VITAMIN B_1), VITAMIN B_{12}, FOLIC ACID AND VITAMIN D.

This term has no legal meaning. The product still may contain preservatives, artificial flavor, and other additives.

The number of calories must be within 20 percent of the actual amount. One ounce of this cereal could contain from 80 to 120 calories.

Sodium is found in more than 70 compounds used in food preparation other than salt. The American Heart Association recommends a daily sodium intake of less than 1000 mg sodium per 1000 calories.

Sugar refers to sucrose, but sugar comes in many forms, which are listed separately on the label: corn syrup, brown sugar, honey, dextrose, maltose, sorbitol, and fructose.

6

BREAKFAST

Many of you have heard the saying, "Eat breakfast like a king, lunch like a queen, and dinner like a pauper." This is very true. If we cannot manage to make our breakfast the biggest meal of the day, then it should be at least one fourth to one third of our total nutritional intake for the day. Do people over age fifty need reminding of the importance of a good breakfast? I am proud to report that skipping breakfast was *not* a big problem at the senior citizen nutrition classes I taught for the last 20 years; however, many of us need reminders of why breakfast *is* the most significant meal of the day, even if only to argue the case with our children and grandchildren, who are notorious for skipping breakfasts.

What are some of the negative effects if we do eliminate the first meal of the day or skimp on a nutritious breakfast? Breakfast, as the name implies, means "breaking the fast." We have not had anything going through our digestive system for at least eight hours. During the night, our blood sugar or (glucose level) falls. If we do not eat the proper foods, this low blood sugar level puts a strain on our body and can cause some serious problems. Fatigue can set in easily, even after a good night's sleep. We are more irritable and our reaction time is slower. In many studies and research, it has been proven that not only is our physical stamina extremely low but our mental capabilities, attention span, and ability to reason are not keen or accurate. Dr. John L. Stanton, Ph.D., of Saint Joseph's University in Philadelphia, did a study on diets of 12,000 people. The study found that people who had cereal for breakfast had the lowest cholesterol levels, whereas the breakfast skippers had the highest. It may not be what's in the cereal, but the fact that people who do eat breakfast are more aware of proper eating habits all day every day. In another study, it was found that breakfast eaters' total fiber intake for the day was higher and their fat consumption lower. Breakfast eaters have a tendency to consume more of the essential nutrients and generally are more resistant to infection and disease.

Another negative is the metabolic slump a breakfast skipper experiences. People who skip breakfast have a metabolic rate about 5 percent lower than normal. This can cause a weight gain. Many times people give the reason for not eating breakfast as due to their being on a diet. What a misconception! Overeating later in the day commonly occurs.

Some of the reasons people give for inadequate breakfast intake are that they do not have time, they are not hungry, breakfast is boring, it makes them feel too bloated, they want to exercise first, they like to sleep late, they get up too early! One of my favorites from one of my students was, "I can't eat my big farmer's breakfast anymore, so I just won't eat *any*." Do you know what his farmer's breakfast was? Two or three fried eggs, plenty of fried bacon, sausage, and ham, fried potatoes, a stack of pancakes with plenty of butter and syrup! Wow, thank goodness everyone knows better now not to eat high-fat, high-cholesterol, high-sodium meals! The majority of people over age fifty do eat breakfast, but their main complaint is they do not have the imagination to think of interesting menus, just the same old standbys.

I am proud of the students I have had in my nutrition classes who are willing to change, use their creativity, and try atypical meals. We should become familiar with planning breakfast as a complete meal, just like our main dinner at night. A proper breakfast should have some fruit, a serving or two from the bread/cereal group, and some protein-rich food. Fruit and fruit juices are easy to start with, vegetables might need a little more thought; bread/cereal group (a natural at breakfast), and dairy fit easily; and don't forget the meat, poultry, fish group. Note, bacon or sausage does not count as a meat, but as a fat. We need the dairy and meat group to provide protein to build up and maintain our blood sugar level.

Here are some tips to help you expand your horizons in the morning or any time of day. Plan ahead. Look at your menu plan the night before. Fix part or all of your breakfast the preceding day. Make a batch of muffins and keep them in the freezer. Try leftovers from the previous evening. Make a healthy liquid shake. Make homemade breakfasts to pop in the microwave. Use yogurt or low-fat cottage cheese instead of milk. Try pita bread, bagels, and tortillas instead of bread. Experiment with different spreads and condiments. Don't always save your fancy new recipes for the weekend, but try something new and different in the middle of the week; join a friend for breakfast. Add your own ideas to this list to make an unusual, innovative breakfast regimen. Enjoy!

7

LUNCH

When I think of lunch, I think of the 3 S's—sandwiches, soups, and salads. Remember, there are no set eating patterns in meal planning. You can eat breakfast at lunch, lunch at breakfast, supper, or dinner, dinner at lunch, and so on. Some people prefer frequent mini-meals or "grazing." Just so all nutrients are included daily. Often lunch is the meal that is ignored or lacks preplanning. Probably one of the reasons we tend not to eat a healthy, balanced lunch is that it sometimes is eaten alone. As we get older, we need to make sure that the food we consume is higher in nutrients but lower in calories than when we were younger. We cannot afford to eat a lot of junk food. To ensure this, write down your lunch menus as well as your dinner and breakfast. Our bodies need adequate fuel for the afternoon, no matter what our job or activities may be.

Many times our lunch habits stem from childhood. I was raised on a farm and I believed my mother lived in the kitchen. Feeding farm help was a big job. A heavy dinner at noon and lunch in midafternoon were both very important. Of course, the meals were huge, too much so for most of our lifestyles today. I can remember the lunch pail lunches at the one-room country school as being very important and the contents delicious and nutritious. Sometimes the lunches included the 3 S's—sandwiches, soup, and salad.

Enough reminiscing. What can we do today to improve our lunches and help us keep fit over age fifty? Here are some ideas to inspire you to diversify your lunch habits.

Sandwiches: Choose a variety of breads: pumpernickel, whole wheat, rye. Try pita bread with a potpourri of fillings. How about a flour tortilla with the meats you would put on bread? If you serve your own lean meats, you will have less fat

31

and sodium than packaged lunch meat and it will be less expensive. Choose natural and low-fat cheeses. Choose different vegetables for your sandwiches besides the standard lettuce and tomato. Chop the vegetables if you have difficulty chewing. Look in your refrigerator to see what leftovers would make a unique sandwich. Be careful of the condiments on sandwiches. Margarine, mayonnaise, and peanut butter are high in fat, and ketchup, mustard, olives, and pickles are high in sodium. They should be used sparingly.

Soups: Many of us in the over fifty crowd grew up on delicious homemade soups. The thermos in my lunch box filled the schoolhouse with a wonderful aroma of the home-made soup-of-the-day. The soup aisle at the grocery store is mind-boggling. Be sure to read the labels carefully because so many commercial soups contain excessive sodium. If you prepare your own, you know what you are getting. Soup making can be a creative art, and economical as well. Soup can be a complete meal in itself. Use your imagination in addition to a favorite recipe if needed. Some suggestions: Have on hand a variety of frozen vegetables, dried foodstuffs such as pasta, rice, beans, and peas, fresh vegetables (like celery, onion), leftovers in your refrigerator and freezer, and a supply of herbs and spices.

Making soup is so individual. You can use canned or dry stock, but be careful that it is not too high in sodium. The ultimate is homemade soup stock. One of the secrets is to use plenty of bones for a rich flavor. Make sure you trim the fat off the meat and use spices and herbs instead of salt for flavoring. Plan ahead so that you can refrigerate the stock for about two days, then skim off the fat so the flavors will be enhanced. For cream soups, use dried, skim milk added just before serving, instead of cream. This way you will get the protein and calcium but not the fat and calories. It tastes great!

Don't forget to experiment with various types of cold soups, or just serve your favorite hot soup chilled for a variation. Use vegetables, cheese, or crackers for toppings. So, next time you are bored or don't know what to serve for lunch or dinner, just holler "Soup's on!"

Salads: Another way to get the four food groups in one dish is to have a salad. You could think of a salad as a sandwich without the bread. Most Americans still are not getting the recommended amounts of fruit and vegetables into their daily diet. A good way to increase this is to have a salad as a main course. A serving of fruits and vegetables is considered one-half cup and you should have at least four servings in this group per day. With both vegetable and fruit salads, you must be very careful that the salad dressing does not contain too much fat, sodium, or sugar.

Vegetable salads are another way to use your imagination. Strolling through the produce department or going to a farmer's market is a real adventure. The wide assortment of fruits and vegetables are now available on a year-round basis. The foundation can be salad greens. It usually is advisable to use the darkest greens, such as spinach; the darker the color, the richer it is in nutrients. Experiment with some of the newer ones, such as endive, bibb, chicory, romaine, and escarole. Add some red and yellow vegetables, an ounce or two of meat or cheese, a sliced hard-boiled egg, some pasta, and you have the four food groups.

Fruit salads are refreshing and just as much fun to make. Take advantage of the new fruits in your market. Keep on hand canned and frozen fruits packed in water or their own juices. Top off your lunch with a delicious red apple, half a grapefruit, orange sections, or a banana, and you will have enough fuel for whatever the afternoon brings.

8

DINNER

If we are to eat dinner like a pauper, what is left? Bread and water? Everyone resists change. Almost everyone is accustomed to having their main meal in the evening. If you are retired or can eat your big meal at noon, it is a worthwhile practice. Can we have our cake and eat it too? Yes, but we must cut down on our portion size in the evening. It can be beneficial to schedule dinner at an earlier hour. As we age, mealtimes become important as a social outlet and we enjoy eating out when possible. Remember though, the healthiest eating will be at *home*. You are in better control in your own kitchen.

It is still important to remember the four food groups for all meals. No matter who does the cooking or what their age, everyone is interested in convenience and ease of preparation. To me, those two terms mean that you do not want to spend more than 30 minutes preparing a meal. With proper planning, efficient grocery shopping, and organization in the kitchen, you can meet that goal. There are so many good planning guides and cookbooks to make dinners quick, easy, and healthy.

Let's examine a typical evening dinner. It will include some type of meat, poultry, or fish, a starch such as potato or rice, a vegetable, a salad, perhaps bread or a roll, and dessert. Will proper nutrition over fifty let us have all of this for an evening dinner? We usually do not require this inclusive a menu for the evening meal as our evening schedule is not as busy as our daytime one. We would be wise as we age to erase the stereotypical important evening meal. Because we require the same number of nutrients but fewer calories as we age, it is very important to make those calories count. Two dinner ideas are tacos and pizza. They both contain something from all four food groups.

When a lot of us were learning to cook, the "in" thing was to make fancy, gourmet dishes. The richer the better, and the more complicated sauces your kitchen produced, the better your cooking reputation. That thinking is now old-fashioned and we must think "simpler is better." Fixing low-fat, low-sodium, low-cholesterol dishes that show a "with it" attitude is an excellent approach to positively influencing our own health as well as our family's. There is absolutely nothing wrong with making that evening meal one of the 3 S's from lunch, or a bowl of cereal or a waffle from breakfast. It is fun to create new and different recipes from leftovers. Use your ingenuity and have a good time.

9

DAIRY

From cradle to rocking chair, dairy products are a vital part of good nutrition. They are an excellent source of calcium and protein, and some believe they are a nearly perfect food. They contain carbohydrates, fat, many of the B vitamins, and other important minerals such as potassium. Most milks are now fortified with vitamins A and D.

What do dairy products do for our body? They help with growth and development, especially of strong bones and healthy teeth. They also help repair and maintain body tissues and organs and increase our energy level.

Are there any negatives in the consumption of dairy products? They can be high in fat and sodium, so it is imperative that you shop wisely. We should strive for a minimum of two servings per day, a serving being one cup of milk or its equivalent. If you are at risk for osteoporosis, at least three servings a day are necessary to meet your calcium requirements.

So join me on our shopping trip at the dairy case. Many stores have the dairy products in two separate places, milk and milk products in one area and other dairy products on another aisle. Let's take a look at the types of milks, cultured milk products, cheeses, and frozen dairy commodities.

There is a big difference in fat and calorie content between skim milk and whole milk. Comparing one cup, skim has 90 calories and 1 gram of fat; low-fat (1 percent) has 105 calories and 2 grams of fat, low-fat (2 percent) has 125 calories and 5 grams of fat; and whole milk has 150 calories and 8 grams of fat. In terms of fat content, there is not a significant difference between whole milk and 2 percent low-fat milk. If you are not used to skim milk, change gradually until you have adjusted to the taste of lower fat milk. We won't even bother discussing cream and half-and-half: just stay away from them, except for special treats. You can, however, try replacing cream with evaporated skim milk. A wholesome and economical milk is dried powdered milk. I keep a box on hand for cooking and even have gotten used to having it on my cereal in the morning. Give it a try. You might learn to like it.

By *cultured dairy products* we mean cottage cheese, sour cream, buttermilk, and yogurt. Cultured milk products are made from fresh dairy milk that has been fermented. They all have a very distinctive flavor. In choosing cottage cheese, make sure that it is 2 percent low fat or less and low sodium. Many companies are producing a sour cream that usually has two thirds less fat and one third fewer calories. Imitation sour creams made with vegetable oil are still high in fat. Another reminder: read those labels. When we think of buttermilk, we think of delicious chocolate cakes! Even though the name has butter in it, that does not imply that it is high in fat. In fact, it is as low in fat as skim milk but is relatively high in sodium. If you don't want to drink it, use it in your favorite salad dressing recipes.

Yogurt has been a staple around the world for centuries, but is relatively new in our culture. It has a higher concentration of calcium than any other dairy product (at 425 mg calcium in 8 ounces of nonfat plain yogurt). It makes an excellent substitute for sour cream, cream cheese, and ricotta cheese. In many recipes that call for milk or sour cream, you can substitute half yogurt for a distinctive flavor. Mix it with fruit to eat alone, or try as a dessert with sponge or angel food cake. It is a good topping for cereal for breakfast or even pie. It also can replace the mayonnaise you use in salads and sandwiches. Try diluting your mayonnaise with yogurt, and slowly wean yourself off the mayonnaise. If you do cook with it, it should be at room temperature. "The sky's the limit" on including yogurt in your menu planning. Here is a chance to try something you may not have eaten when you were growing up.

We could devote a whole Key to cheeses. Natural cheeses made with part skim milk are somewhat lower in fat than those made with whole milk. Processed American cheese, cheese food, and cheese spreads are lower in calcium and much higher in sodium than most natural cheeses. Practically every week a new cheese product that is lower in calories, fat, and sodium comes on the market. Cheese should remain a part of your diet, but make sure that the percentage of fat is not too high. The rule of thumb is, it is okay if it's less than 2 grams of fat per ounce.

Oh, for a scoop of old-fashioned homemade ice cream! This is a tradition at our house on the Fourth of July. Thank goodness there are some pretty good substitutes in the ice cream case today, considering that we need to watch our fat intake. Think of frozen dairy products on the same scale as milk. There is sorbet, sherbet, ice milk, regular ice cream, gourmet ice cream, and frozen yogurt. Sorbets are made from fruit juices without milk. Sherbet is sometimes made with milk, egg whites, and/or gelatin. It can be low in calories but also lowest in calcium. Naturally the more butterfat in ice cream the higher the fat and calorie content, but also the more calcium. Frozen yogurt can be a healthy substitute depending on some variables. It is not as dense in nutrients as regular yogurt, but can be a nice change of pace when you have a craving for something cold and creamy.

A negative to dairy products as we age is lactose intolerance. We will discuss that in Key 38, Digestive Diseases/Disorders/Deficiencies. When you are at the dairy case, be selective, and read those labels!

10

CALCIUM/OSTEOPOROSIS

Peak bone mass is thought to be reached around 21 years of age. Then, until the age of thirty-five, the bone mass may not increase, but is maintained. After the age of thirty-five a little more bone is lost than is gained. Bones maintain themselves throughout life by a process known as remodeling. That is, small amounts of old bone are removed and new bone is formed in its place. Osteoporosis literally means "porous bone." There is a thinning and increased porosity of bones, causing weaker bones that are more susceptible to fractures. Some health care experts believe osteoporosis has reached epidemic proportions. It is basically a woman's issue, but because men are living longer it also can affect men, usually about ten years later than women.

Osteoporosis is sometimes called the "silent disease" because there are no true signs of the onset until the bone loss sometimes reaches as much as 25 percent. Some of the warnings are as follows: a shrinking of body height, frequent backaches, a curving of the spine or "dowager's hump," and fractures, commonly in the spine, wrist, and hip. Several methods for diagnosing osteoporosis are available, such as X rays and new sophisticated machines that can evaluate the density of the bones.

There are several risk factors that make a person more prone to the disease. Assess your potential vulnerability after reading this list: being a woman, especially with early menopause, being Caucasian, having a family history of osteoporosis, being on the thin side, having a low intake of calcium, consuming large amounts of protein, smoking cigarettes, drinking alcohol and caffeine excessively, and not exercising regularly. These are the most common risk factors. How did you do?

Because this book pertains to the over fifty crowd, I am sure you found some risk factors pertinent to you.

In general, as both women and men age, their bodies begin to absorb less calcium. This begins at about age forty-five for women and age sixty for men.

The role of estrogen, the female hormone, is very influential in controlling the cessation or slowing down of bone loss. It is extremely important for all women to be aware of their biological clock and seek advice on what is best for them. Each person has to be treated according to individual risk factors. Estrogen replacement therapy is being recommended by many doctors. It tends to slow down but not reverse osteoporosis.

If there is no cure and no adequate treatment for everyone, what can we do for prevention or to at least retard bone loss? If you review the risks, some of them just require a change in lifestyle. The biggest favor you can do for yourself is to have a regular exercise program. Lack of exercise can cause an incredible bone loss at a accelerated rate. If you were to rest in bed for a month, you could lose as much at 4 percent of your bone mass. Regular exercise is absolutely critical for strong, healthy bones. It is believed that exercise can halt bone loss and perhaps stimulate the formation of new bone. It should be weight-bearing exercise, such as walking, to stress the long bones. The minimum time devoted to this program should be 30 minutes three times per week.

What role does nutrition play in the whole picture of osteoporosis? A very important role. The bones and teeth contain about 99 percent of the calcium in the body. The body keeps a relatively constant level of calcium in the blood. So besides being important to building and maintaining strong bones, calcium has other vital jobs to perform. It contributes to contraction of muscles, beating of the heart, and clotting of blood. When the blood calcium level drops, more calcium is taken out of the bones to maintain the appropriate level in the blood. As we age, the absorption of calcium is not as efficient and we tend to consume less calcium in our diet. Although much research is constantly being done on the amount we need, it is believed that we need somewhere between 1,000 and 1,500 milligrams of calcium per day.

The major source of calcium in an American diet is dairy products. They provide more than 70 percent of our supply of calcium. Other foods rich in this mineral are fish with bones and dark green vegetables. One cup of 1 percent low-fat milk contains 300 mg of calcium, one cup of plain yogurt, 415 mg; one ounce of Swiss cheese, 272 mg; 3 ounces sardines (with bones), 371 mg; one cup cooked broccoli, raw 136 mg, frozen 100 mg; one cup collards (chopped and cooked), 357 mg. I suggest you get a calcium food chart and keep track daily of your calcium intake for a week or two to evaluate your calcium intake. Do you get approximately 1,000 milligrams per day without trying? If not, could you get enough simply by adding one more serving of milk or yogurt? If dairy products are a problem for you, you may need to rely on a supplement for part of or all of your calcium needs. Make an effort to add calcium rich foods to your means. One quick and easy way that I have found is to add nonfat dry milk to almost everything you prepare. Also, do not overload your diet with protein because that causes excess excretion of calcium.

Another area to be aware of is adequate vitamin D, which is necessary for the proper absorption of calcium. The main sources are from sunlight and fortified milk. The right balance of phosphorus also is necessary but it is so widely available in foods that we usually do not have to be concerned.

We will discuss calcium supplements in the Key on minerals. Please consult a doctor, registered dietitian, and nutritionist to help you understand this debilitating condition and to assist you in seeking information to help you have the right balance of nutrients in your diet and an adequate supply of calcium from natural food sources.

11

MEAT/POULTRY/FISH/EGGS

Now that we have done an A+ job selecting just the right dairy products, let's wander over to the meat counter. Do you recall going to the neighborhood meat market? The butcher was a well-respected friend. You knew he had the finest quality products available and he knew how to process them. Being a home economics graduate from Iowa State makes me more conscious of selecting good quality meats.

Meat, poultry, fish, eggs, dried lentils, beans, and peas are part of the protein group. This group builds and repairs all of the body tissues and contributes to the production of hormones and enzymes. It also helps maintain the proper balance of fluid in various parts of the body and helps the body resist infection. Probably the best quality protein for building and repairing tissues is the meat group. Being a high density nutrient, it is rich in iron, zinc, and the B vitamins. We want to aim for no more than 3–4 ounces from meat or other protein equivalents daily.

Meat: Fifty or more years ago, meat was associated with affluence and if you had money you ate a lot of meat. Thus, we overate from that group and skimped on the other food groups. Now we know that this group is important, but not the most important. A good rule of thumb is to consume about 3 ounces of red meat no more than three times a week (4 ounces uncooked). A 3-ounce portion is about the size of a deck of cards. Note: Portion sizes are still in debate.

What has happened in the meat industry? The beef, veal, pork, and lamb produced today are all more lean, containing less fat than they did in the 1950s. The good news is you do not have to cut out, just cut down, on the consumption of beef and the other red meats. The cut, label, and grade are factors to take into consideration. Most beef is now about 25 percent leaner because of crossbreeding stock and finding ways to use younger animals, which still provides good flavor and tenderness. Ask the butcher at your grocery store to explain the various cuts of beef and reacquaint you with the new meat. Look for labels that say *lean* or *extra lean*. Grading is standard and *prime* has the highest content of fat, *choice* grade has less, and *select* is probably the healthiest choice. Remember, red meat includes pork, veal, and lamb too. Even though the meat from those animals is now more wholesome, it is wise to limit the consumption of them to no more than three times a week. If you are unsure of a portion's weight, use a scale to weigh the meat before preparing it. We will discuss preparation, which is equally important, in Key 31, Modifying Recipes/Cooking Methods.

Because I live "out west," a discussion of the benefits of buffalo or bison is in order. Studies show that buffalo has more protein and less cholesterol than other meats, and has only 45 calories per ounce. It is an ideal alternative to beef, especially if you are allergic to beef, or if you are following a low-fat, low-cholesterol, low-calorie diet.

Poultry: In recent years, the poultry family has gotten both good and bad press. It definitely does not have as much fat ingrained into the muscle fiber as red meats. Most of the fat in chicken lies directly beneath the skin and dark meat contains more fat than white. Chicken and turkey have become as versatile in cooking as ground beef. In any recipe that calls for ground beef, you easily can substitute ground turkey or chicken. This is both economical and healthful. Younger poultry is leaner and has less fat than older poultry. The variety at the poultry counter is amazing, ranging from whole fryers to individual pieces, and to the ultimate, but more expensive, boneless, skinless chicken breasts. The controversy that has been provoked stems from the use of chemicals in raising poultry, and in the manner in which poultry is processed and brought to market. Industry regulations are now intact and the consumer should be able to trust them. Key 30 discusses the food safety issue further.

Fish: The popularity and consumption of fish is expanding. Most fish and shell fish are low in total fat, especially in saturated fat. A major health benefit of fish comes from a special kind of polyunsaturated fat known as omega-3 fatty acids. Omega-3 fatty acids interfere with the buildup of plaque in the blood vessels. Many health care professionals recommend that fish be eaten two to three times a week. Perhaps in your store you will find the fish in two separate places, the frozen in one area and the fresh at another.

My first memory of fish was on our farm when the mobile ice cream truck also sold fish! Our ice cream cones always tasted like fish and we were uneasy about buying the fish, not knowing its freshness. We have seen much progress, haven't we?

Many of us in the fifty-plus group have to relearn how to buy and prepare fish, as this has changed a great deal in the last decade. Seafood offers us the most varied selection of any food in the protein group. Because of the advances in raising and processing, we are getting a finer quality fish today. When purchasing fish, make sure to buy from a store with a reputation for high standards. Use your senses of sight and smell when choosing fish. The skin should look and feel moist and shiny, and it should not have a sharp fishy odor. Make sure to refrigerate it immediately after purchasing, and then use it within two days. Clean it thoroughly before cooking by rinsing in cold water and using very clean utensils.

Many recipes can be adapted to using fish instead of meat or poultry. Like meat and poultry, for health reasons, it is best to broil, poach, steam, grill, or bake fish. A good rule to follow is to cook fish at a high temperature, ten minutes for each inch of thickness.

Eggs: Eggs often are classified in the dairy group and also in the meat group. The amount of eggs in a healthy diet is a controversial subject. From previously eating eggs daily, we now are cautioned to eat no more than one or none a week, or at the most three per week. Eggs are an excellent source of protein, vitamins, and minerals and improve the taste and texture of many baked goods and other food products. If a reduction in the intake of eggs is recommended, there are now egg substitutes that have been developed, which are very adequate for eating and cooking. You can make your own egg substitute by using two egg whites instead of one whole egg. This costs less than the products at the store. To achieve a healthier product, many recipes suggest using more egg whites than yolks. So, it is possible to "have your cake and eat it too!" Only you and your health care professional can decide what is the best course of action. Be sure to take note of egg safety in Key 30.

My personal philosophy for this food group is to encourage limiting animal protein to about 3 ounces per day, varying the menus, and making sure that the recipes and cooking methods used are wholesome.

12

FATS/OILS/CHOLESTEROL

Do we actually go shopping for fat and is it considered a food group in this day and age? Yes and no. Fats are hidden in many foods. Fat is found with protein and some carbohydrates as well as in its pure form. I like to consider it in the "other" category. Fat serves a multitude of important roles and we could not survive without it. It is a major source of energy and adds flavor and variety to our foods. Fat also protects the heart, kidneys, liver, and other body organs and is essential for the proper functioning of our bodies. Fat carries and helps absorb the fat-soluble vitamins A, D, E, and K. It is the most concentrated source of food energy (calories). Each gram of fat supplies about 9 calories, compared with protein or carbohydrates, which supplies 4 calories per gram.

We already have discussed the importance of choosing low-fat products in the protein groups (dairy, meat, poultry, and fish). Fatty acids are the basic chemical units in fat. There are saturated, monounsaturated, or polyunsaturated fats. All dietary fats are a mixture of these three types. Saturated fats and cholesterol can cause elevated blood cholesterol in many people, increasing their risk of heart disease.

The American Heart Association and the American Dietetic Association suggest it is best to limit fat to no more than 30 percent of total calories per day, 10 percent from each of the three types of fats (saturated, monounsaturated, and polyunsaturated). How does the average person apply this to his or her daily diet? If you read labels and choose products that are in the range of 2–3 grams of fat per serving, you're doing fine. If a product has 10–15 grams of fat per serving, you better think twice about consuming that particular product.

Saturated fats primarily come from animal products but also are found in tropical plants, such as coconut and palm.

Monounsaturated fats are found in oils (liquid at room temperature), and are derived from vegetables, such as peanuts or olives. *Polyunsaturated fats* are found in vegetable oils, such as canola, safflower, corn, and soybean. We want to be aware of the polyunsaturated fats that help lower blood cholesterol levels and the saturated fats that raise blood cholesterol levels.

Hydrogenated fats are oils that have been hardened into solids and in the process have become saturated. Vegetable shortening and margarines are made from liquid plant oils that have gone through a process called hydrogenation. This process changes the original poly or mono unsaturated oil to a more saturated oil. It makes the product soft or hard at room temperature depending on the extent of hydrogenation. This process extends the product's shelf life. So, vegetable shortening is not necessarily better for you than animal lard, just because the fat came from a vegetable. Margarines are still less saturated than butter and do not contain cholesterol.

What is *cholesterol?* It is a waxy, fat-like substance carried in the bloodstream. Your body manufactures all the cholesterol you need for the production of cells and hormones. It also helps metabolize fat and insulates nerves. There are two forms, high density lipoproteins (HDL) the "good" cholesterol, and low density lipoproteins (LDL) or the "bad" cholesterol. The bad cholesterol leads to a buildup on artery walls, restricting the flow of blood, and the good cholesterol helps keep the arteries clean. Authorities generally have agreed that a cholesterol reading 200 mg or higher can be a cause for concern. What is important is the ratio of the "good" cholesterol to the "bad." Monounsaturated fats lower the bad cholesterol without lowering the good cholesterol.

Dietary cholesterol is not to be confused with your own body's cholesterol. It is not quite the villain that it has been made out to be. Of the cholesterol you consume each day, only about 40 percent of it actually is absorbed by the digestive system. The amount of cholesterol your body produces is far greater than that which you get from your diet. Cholesterol is only present in animal products. So when you find a label of peanut butter or margarine that claims "no cholesterol," it's true, but only because it never had any. Don't fall prey to the popular gimmick of labels that read "no cholesterol," even when they are high in fat. What's more important than the amount of cholesterol in your diet is the amount of fat, because a diet high in fat (particularly saturated fat) can result in higher blood cholesterol.

Reading labels is crucial when shopping for fats and oils and products that contain fats. Generally a product is low in fat if it has less than 2–3 grams of fat per serving. Many nutritional labels on packaged foods show the amount of unsaturated and saturated fatty acids and the amount of cholesterol they contain. Check the type of fat on the label. Is it high in saturated fat? Or is it high in polyunsaturated fat? Is it partially hydrogenated or hydrogenated? Choose a product with the lowest proportion of saturated fat. Remember, labels that read "cholesterol-free" still may be high in fat.

Learn to use all fat and oil products sparingly when cooking and eating. Use unsaturated vegetable oils and margarines made with liquid vegetable oils for spreads and dressings and in baking when possible. Try the no-stick sprays available with lecithin, corn oil, or olive oil; they are considered safe. Further, choose one in a pump container rather than in an aerosol can (to spare our atmosphere).

Use the oil-free or polyunsaturated salad dressings or "light" mayonnaise, which has less than half the fat of regular mayonnaise. Or substitute some of the mayonnaise with yogurt. Now there is even fat-free mayonnaise.

Short-term studies and longer-term research clearly are warranted on these complicated and constantly changing issues. We will be mentioning fat in some form or other throughout this entire book. Keep up with all of the information available. In the meantime, moderation is the key word. It is a real challenge to go grocery shopping in this aisle.

13

VITAMINS

For older adults, decreased caloric requirements and assuring food sources rich in nutrients are vital, but, as of this writing, suggested daily requirements for most vitamins and minerals remain essentially the same for older person as for younger adults. There is not a lot of information on the specific vitamin and mineral needs of the older adult.

Some medications and chronic disorders may interfere with the metabolism and absorption of vitamins and minerals in older adults. Long- or short-term illnesses can put stress on the body and may deplete whatever stores exist. It is imperative that we treat each person individually when assessing vitamin and mineral requirements.

Vitamins are activators for important body functions. The fat-soluble vitamins (A, D, E, K) are metabolized by fat and bile, and are stored in the body. The water-soluble vitamins (C, B complex) must be replenished constantly because they are not stored in the body. With the recent abuse of vitamin C supplementation in the past decade, researchers have noted that vitamin C can accumulate in the body and may be involved with oxylic kidney stones. If we follow closely the RDA (Recommended Daily Allowances) of the food groups, shop wisely, use the proper cooking techniques, and eat a variety of food, then we probably will have also met the daily requirements for vitamins and minerals. The body only needs small amounts of all vitamins.

Vitamin A: Another name for vitamin A is retinol, which is supplied mainly by foods of animal origin. It is found in large quantities in liver, fortified milk, cheese, and egg yolks. Vitamin A promotes bone and tooth development, is important for night vision, keeps skin and mucous membranes healthy, and helps fight infections.

Vegetables contain substances called carotenes, which are converted into vitamin A in the body. Beta carotene is found in abundance in orange-red vegetables, such as carrots, squash, and pumpkin, and in high quantities in green leafy vegetables. Fruits high in vitamin A are cantaloupe and apricots. Although Vitamin A is stored in the body, you will not obtain toxic levels of it from food. You get vitamin A in your diet in a previtamin form called beta carotene and your body only converts what it needs to vitamin A.

Vitamin D: Vitamin D increases the amount of calcium absorption and maintains bone density. It is important in the prevention of osteoporosis. It is found in fortified dairy products, margarine, and fish oils. Older adults can get adequate amounts both through food and by being in the sun about 15 minutes a day.

Vitamin E: This vitamin protects body tissues from damage, protects vitamins A, C, and unsaturated fatty acids in food against oxidation, and prevents destruction of red blood cells and essential fatty acids. It is found in vegetable oils and margarine, green and leafy vegetables, wheat germ and whole grain products, liver, and egg yolk. Claims of the success of vitamin E in diminishing the aging process and working other so-called miracles have not been proved.

Vitamin K: This vitamin plays an essential role in assisting blood clotting. It is produced naturally by bacteria in the intestines. The major food sources for vitamin K are dark green leafy vegetables, liver, and soybean and corn oils. Blood thinners are anticoagulants. Vitamin K is a coagulant. A supplement may be very dangerous!

Vitamin C: We automatically think of vitamin C when fighting a cold. But controversy still continues on this subject. We do know that we need it to improve the assimilation and efficiency of iron, to aid in healing wounds, help bone and tooth formation, and strengthen blood vessel walls. The most concentrated form is in citrus fruits. Other foods containing vitamin C are tomatoes, dark green vegetables, potatoes, broccoli, and strawberries.

Vitamin B Complex: As the name implies, this is a composite of eight water-soluble vitamins: thiamin (B_1), riboflavin (B_2), niacin (B_3), pyridoxine (B_6), B_{12}, folic acid, biotin, and pantothenic acid. They are all water-soluble and are excreted from the body if not used. Dietary deficiencies of this group are unusual. They function as coenzymes and assist the body in obtaining energy from food. They also promote good vision, healthy skin, and red blood cell formation. Because of the enrichment of refined grains and grain products, the essential B complex nutrients are put back into processed foods. Again, if you eat a variety from all of the food groups, you will obtain sufficient vitamins in this group, even though absorption does slow down with age.

B complex and C vitamins are water-soluble and need to be replaced every day because they are not stored in the body, but are eliminated in your urine. You need to have sufficient quantities of these daily.

A few words about vitamin supplements. This is an individual matter depending on such things as your overall health, lifestyle, age, body size, genetics, and climate and how you shop, prepare food, and eat. Remember, as we age, there is a lower percentage of lean muscle and a greater percentage of body fat. If we do not remain active, the importance of eating nutrient-dense foods intensifies. It can be difficult to constantly get adequate vitamins and minerals. I take a multivitamin supplement so that I am assured of a balanced amount. A multivitamin is safer than individual vitamins, and one multivitamin every other day may be all you need. One vitamin in particular to watch out for in supplement form is vitamin A. One can build up a toxic amount of vitamin A because there is an increased ability to store it and a decreased ability to remove it from storage in the older individual. There is no guarantee that increasing vitamins will give you perfect health, prevent illnesses, or cure diseases.

14

MINERALS

Even though most supermarkets have shelves devoted to supplemental vitamins and minerals, my hope is that all of you are making a conscientious effort to obtain these substances through the food products you consume.

What are minerals? They are in organic substances that perform a variety of important functions in the body. Like vitamins, we could not survive without them. There are two kinds of minerals, the macrominerals and the microminerals or trace minerals. The macro are needed in larger amounts and the micro are equally important, but we need only very minute quantities. The seven macrominerals are calcium, sodium, potassium, magnesium, phosphorus, chlorine, and sulfur. Calcium was discussed in Keys 9 and 10 and we will discuss sodium in Keys 24 and 42. The 14 trace minerals are iron, zinc, selenium, copper, manganese, fluorine, iodine, chromium, tin, silicon, vanadium, molybdenum, cobalt, and nickel. Most of these 21 minerals do not need individual attention as we age. We just need to know that if we eat a variety of fresh foods, prepare them properly and eat the recommended daily allowance, we will not have to worry about mineral deficiencies.

However, some of these minerals are of more importance as we grow older, due to inadequate nutrition, poor absorption, chronic illnesses, age-associated diseases, or medicine and drug interactions. Sometimes iron intake can be low in older adults. Iron is essential for the formation of hemoglobin, which carries oxygen in the red blood cells. Iron has the ability to be stored in the body. We think of iron needs during growth or periods of blood loss, especially with females. But both sexes require iron, and senior citizens should eat iron-rich foods. Vitamin C, eaten along with iron-rich foods, will increase the absorption of iron. Some good sources of iron are liver, all of the meat, poultry, and fish group, whole grain and enriched breads and cereals, and iron-fortified breads and cereals. Plant sources of iron include dried beans, peas, lentils, greens, apricots, dates, raisins, and prunes.

Potassium and magnesium are the two main minerals within our body cells. They are important for proper muscle and nerve functioning. They also help with energy production. Potassium works with sodium and chloride to maintain the proper water balance. Sometimes frequent use by the fifty-plus crowd of diuretics, laxatives, aspirin, and other drugs can lead to a depletion of potassium. Sources of potassium are potatoes, bananas, greens, broccoli, milk, tomatoes, grapefruit, and oranges.

Magnesium assists in energy production and protein formation and activates many enzymes. It works very closely with calcium and phosphorus. The greatest concentration of magnesium is in the bones with some in muscle, soft tissue, and body fluids. It is possible to have a deficiency of magnesium if you have too high an intake of calcium, consume too much alcohol, have had surgery or liver or kidney disease, or take diuretics. Magnesium is found in fish, green vegetables, whole grains, eggs, and nuts.

Another highly publicized mineral we need is zinc. Zinc promotes the healing of wounds and the functioning of enzymes that make all of the metabolic systems function efficiently. It plays an important role in our ability to taste and smell. It aids in building a strong immune system to fight infections. Zinc can be acquired by eating peas, whole grain cereals, liver, oysters, corn, peanut butter, and milk.

The key to adequate vitamins and minerals is to eat a variety of foods. Do not be fooled by false claims of miracle cures, but keep abreast of the latest research. On the following page is a reference chart, "Nutrient Needs For Seniors," developed by Tamara Nelson, M.S., R.D., a geriatric dietitian.

So, where do we go from here? Let's see what the produce department has to offer.

NUTRIENT NEEDS FOR SENIORS

Nutrient RDA*	Proposed Changes for Seniors	Good Food Sources	Deficiency
Vitamin A 800–1,000 RE	Less: can build up to toxic amounts when taken by supplement	Liver, egg yolk, milk, butter, dark green and deep yellow vegetables	Not likely to be deficient Avoid supplement >1,000 RE vitamin A
Vitamin B$_6$ 1.6–2.0 mg	More: risk for and more sensitive to depletion	Yeast, wheat germ, pork, liver, legumes, potatoes, bananas, whole grain cereals, and breads	Anemia, weakness, nervousness, insomnia, glossitis, and poor immune function
Folic acid 180–200 mcg	More: higher amount than RDA due to poor intake	Same as Vitamin B$_6$ foods, plus green leafy vegetables, broccoli, asparagus, and nuts	Anemia/poor quality red blood cells, glossitis (swollen tongue)
Vitamin B$_{12}$	More: due to low intake in diet and poor absorption	Meat, eggs, cheese, fish, or 3 ounces of liver once a month	Anemia, unsteady gait, lethargy
Vitamin C 60 mg	More: due to low intake in diet	Strawberries, broccoli, orange, brussel sprouts, green pepper, cantaloupe, and cabbage	Poor wound healing and resistance to infection, poor iron absorption
Vitamin D 200 I.U. or 5 mcg	More: 400 I.U. or 10 mcg due to less time spent outdoors	Expose arms and face to sun 20 minutes twice a week, Vitamin D fortified milk	Necessary for absorption of calcium
Calcium 800 mg	More: 1,000–1,500 mg due to poor intestinal absorption	3–4 dairy servings per day milk, cheese, yogurt, ice cream	Osteoporosis, adequate calcium will slow bone loss
Zinc 12–15 mg	More: due to low intake in diet	Animal protein, particularly fish and seafood	Poor immune function, loss of appetite, and possibly taste
Water	Risk for dehydration due to an impaired sense of thirst	6–8 cups fluids per day milk, juice, jello, herb teas, water	Confused state

*RDA = Recommended Daily Allowances

At this time, specific amounts necessary for older persons are not known. The proposed changes are listed for some vitamins. For others, only the general change of "more" or "less" is known.

15

VEGETABLES

How many times do you recall your grandmother, your mother, and then yourself saying, "Eat your vegetables. They're good for you." This is wise and true advice! In the days of the large home gardens, when harvest time came, many types of vegetables were eaten in a single meal, yet you did not consider yourself a vegetarian. Since the "olden days," we progressed to canned corn, canned green beans, and canned peas, the extent of our vegetable selection.

Today, venturing into the produce department at the supermarket is like going into a candy store. There is such a tempting variety to choose from! It is called a department, not a counter or an aisle, because that is how extensive and important it is. Instead of rushing through the produce section, take time to notice the wide variety there is to choose from. Some of the items are so new that we do not know if they are fruits or vegetables, what they are used for, and how to prepare them. You can ask the manager of produce, who is usually very knowledgeable and helpful. Many produce departments have on display the nutritional information for each selection.

Using all your senses is important and fun when shopping for produce. Notice the many different colors, almost every color of the rainbow, and the different intensities and hues. Enjoy the various smells, and then think about the sounds the vegetables will make as you are eating them. Imagine the distinctive taste of each vegetable.

Vegetable gardening could be a whole book by itself. It often is pursued as a hobby, for economy, and for the assurance that you are getting a fresh, natural product for your table. In your leisure years, gardening can be very rewarding as you plant and tend your garden. It is good exercise, too! Even though I grew up on a farm, it is my husband who is the gardener in our family. His is a labor of love. We enjoy the fresh produce and freeze some of it for future use.

It is difficult to classify vegetables because of the wide variety available today, but we think of the yellow-orange, cabbage-like, and green leafy, as just three groups of many, many from which we can select. Generally speaking, it is advisable to eat at least three to five servings of vegetables daily. A serving size is usually one-half cup cooked or one cup raw.

Complex carbohydrates occur naturally in vegetables and provide the most nutrients for day-to-day energy. Vegetables also supply a good amount of the necessary vitamins and minerals, especially vitamins A and C. There is continuing research on the significance of the cancer prevention qualities of vegetables. The importance of fiber in the diet is of prime importance and is a good reason to eat those veggies. I suggest that you try and eat at least 60 percent of your vegetables raw, if there is no problem with chewing and digesting, for overcooking can destroy a great amount of their nutrients. Thus you will get the maximum vitamins, minerals, and fiber.

Let's explore the green leafy vegetable counter. What an array to choose from! The general guideline is that the darker the green, the more vitamins and minerals it contains. Learn to use spinach, kale, romaine, both green and red leaf lettuce, greens, and bibb lettuce. Mix the strong, more bitter greens, such as watercress, endive, arugula, radicchio, chicory, escarole, or swiss chard, with the milder types, and don't forget to eat your parsley. It is not just a decoration on your plate!

Cruciferous or crunchy type vegetables have been heralded in recent years for their cancer-fighting properties. Recipes abound for using cabbage, broccoli, cauliflower, and brussels sprouts. Always include some of them on your grocery list and in your shopping cart.

We have been taught that the yellow and orange vegetables contain beta carotene, which has the ability to be converted to vitamin A in the body. It also is being associated with fighting cancer. Carrots are a versatile vegetable in this group. They can be used alone or in combination with other foods. They are excellent served as a condiment instead of pickles and olives, which are salty. Also, do not overlook sweet potatoes and acorn squash in the yellow-orange group.

The challenge of finding a perfect tomato is still with us, whether from the home garden or the produce department. Advances in growing and shipping techniques are improving the quality of this useful and tasteful fruit. Include it for flavor, color, and especially for vitamins A and C, as well as the B vitamins and essential minerals.

With my name being Murphy, we must investigate the potato! It is a food that can fit into several other groups, (especially the starch group). It is easy to prepare and usable in many ways, often as a main dish. It is high in fiber, vitamin C, iron, and potassium, and low in fat, if you are cautious about what you add to it! Corn is higher in starch and harder to digest than potatoes, but is good for you in small quantities as you grow older.

Other suggestions are turnips or rutabagas, eggplant, okra, onions, peppers, cucumbers, beets, radishes, mushrooms, alfalfa and bean sprouts, and on and on. So, exercise your imagination, explore, and experiment with the interesting world of vegetables.

16

FRUITS

The fruits are in the simple carbohydrate category and are considered the "good" sugars that provide you so much energy. In a survey it was found that the majority of fruit is eaten for snacks, then lunch, breakfast, and dinner. It can be used for a salad or dessert. There are as many types of fruit as there are vegetables, with new varieties coming on the market all the time. Groupings include citrus, berries, and melons. The most popular are bananas, apples, and seedless grapes.

Most people enjoy eating a variety of fruit, but its consumption is still too low and we must make a concerted effort to increase our daily intake. We should strive for two to four servings per day, a serving being one-half to one cup.

If we have a craving for sweets, fruit is the thing to eat. It has a natural sweetness and we do not have to add refined and processed sugar. If we gradually wean ourselves from artificial sugars, we will be very satisfied with fruit for dessert.

When selecting fresh fruit, make sure there are no signs of bruising. If they are ripe, they should be stored in the refrigerator and used within a few days. Some fruit, such as apples, keep fresh for a longer period. To prevent vitamin loss, serve fruit immediately after preparation and eat it unpeeled whenever possible, but wash it first.

During peak season, make an outing to a farmers' market or stop at produce stands when you're traveling. It's fun to see what is available in different parts of the country and world.

Citrus fruits consist of oranges, grapefruit, lemons, and limes. They are a good source of vitamin C. This group also contains some vitamin A and potassium. The most popular type of orange is the navel. It is seedless, easy to peel, with sections that separate easily. This is important, as even the task of getting a piece of fruit ready to eat can be difficult if you have arthritis in your hands. Vitamin C is not stored in your body, so it is a good idea to include citrus fruit in your daily meal plans.

The berry family consists of over ten different kinds. They are exceptionally high in fiber and have a diversity of uses. They vary widely in taste and texture, from very sweet to extremely sour, from soft to firm. Some are common, others unusual. You can put "berries" as a suffix to all of these: blue, boysen, cran, dew, elder, goose, huckle, logan, rasp, straw. Many of them are wonderful on your favorite cereal, or as a snack or dessert. Kiwi fruit is actually in the berry family. Once exotic, it is now common. Some can be found growing wild and berry picking can be an interesting project. If you have difficulty digesting berries because of the seeds, choose seedless fruit.

Like the vegetable group, there are the more common fruits, such as apples, peaches, melons, and so on. However, if you are bored with the usual and want to try something new, buy one of the exotic fruits. Most of them can now be found in your local produce department. Have you heard these names—cactus pear, plantain, camu camu, jicama, red banana, passion fruit, chayote? Some are classified as both a vegetable and a fruit.

You get the best nutritional advantage from eating your fruit fresh and raw. Then in decreasing order of value from frozen, canned, and dried fruits. Dried fruits have the highest concentration of sugar, but what would we do without raisins, dried apricots, prunes, and dates? If we always ate fresh fruit we wouldn't have to read labels. If you choose a juice, read the label very carefully and make sure the highest content is pure juice and does not include additives. That old saying, "An apple a day keeps the doctor away," is a good practice.

17

FIBER

How many times in the vegetable and fruit Keys was the word fiber mentioned? Frequently! Dietary fiber is from plants; our bodies do not digest it. The role of fiber, bulk, or roughage in the diet always has been important. With scientists and nutritionists constantly doing research, it is still a controversial subject, like so many areas of nutrition. The National Cancer Institute recommends that we obtain between 20 and 35 grams of fiber a day from our diet. Even with a balanced diet, many older Americans are only getting half that amount. It takes real effort to make certain you increase your intake of naturally occurring fiber.

Dietary fiber can be found in all of the carbohydrate food groups. It can be found in vegetables, fruits, pure whole grains, and in breads, cereals, and pastas made from whole grains. It also is found in legumes (beans), nuts, and seeds.

There are two types of fiber: insoluble and soluble. We need both kinds for good health. Water-insoluble fibers are non-digestible. This is the part of a plant that gives it structure and allows it to grow extremely tall. These fibers increase the weight and bulk of the food, thus decreasing the amount of time it takes food to move through the digestive system. It helps prevent constipation and other digestive and bowel problems. There have been studies to indicate a correlation between reducing the risk of colon cancer and the intake of insoluble fiber.

Water-soluble fiber helps to slow down passage of food to the large intestine and increases rate of absorption. Plants can contain some soluble and insoluble fiber. Studies have implied a relationship between major health problems and a reduced intake of soluble fiber. This can become an increased problem for people over fifty. It is believed that a diet high in this type of fiber can lower cholesterol, thus controlling or preventing heart disease. There is some evidence it can play a slight role in controlling diabetes.

We do not need to concern ourselves about what type of fiber we are eating, just so we make a concerted attempt to eat foods high in all types of fiber. Many labels now list the amount of fiber in the product. Increasing your intake of high fiber foods has other benefits as well. It can induce a feeling of fullness; you usually are more satisfied when eating high fiber foods. It requires more chewing (good exercise)! High fiber foods usually are very low in fat and are a wise choice if you are on a weight loss program and want to stabilize your body weight.

Now that we know the importance of fiber, what are some effortless approaches to a high fiber diet? Select proper foods. Make sure they are fresh. Read labels. Try and leave the skins on vegetables and fruits. Eat more seeds and nuts. Cook with legumes and lentils. You probably can furnish additional suggestions and ideas.

So, is more actually better? Should we take a fiber supplement? Like all philosophy in this book, variety, moderation, and balance are the key words. If you consume an excess of fiber, it can decrease the body's absorption of such minerals as calcium and iron. It can cause an imbalance of your digestive system and intestinal functioning. You should only consider fiber supplements when a doctor recommends it and supervises the amount to be taken.

Hopefully we have plenty of fiber in our grocery cart. Let's proceed to the other high fiber sections, which we can find in several areas of the store.

18

GRAIN PRODUCTS

Included in this large classification of grain products are breads, cereals, and pastas. Grain products supply starch, protein, iron, and many of the B vitamins. Whole grain food-stuffs are also good sources of fiber, minerals, and, if they are enriched, can even be more valuable sources of dense nutrients. At least six or more servings per day are recommended. A serving is one slice of bread, $1/2$ to $1 1/2$ cups cereal (exceptions are grapenuts $1/4$ cup and puffed cereals $1 1/2$ cups), or $1/2$ cup of pasta. As you can see, it is fairly easy to get that amount in our daily diet. In my college foods and nutrition classes more than 30 years ago, this group had a bad reputation. The common saying was, "If you want to lose weight, stay away from this group, it's fattening." Now we know just the opposite is true. In their natural state, grains contain very little fat and gram per gram contain less than half the calories of the fat group.

Much is being written about bran. Bran is the protective outer layer of the seed of the grain. That is where the valuable high fiber content exists. Some of the soluble fiber brans are oat, soy, barley, and psyllium. These have been touted as effective in lowering cholesterol. Whole wheat always has been proclaimed a wonderful health food. It is an insoluble fiber but does improve bowel function and is being proclaimed as reducing cancer risk.

There is a wide selection of whole grains to choose from. Some of them were used extensively in ancient times, some of our grandmothers used them, and others are new to our grocery shelf and kitchen. Join me in exploring the old and new grains. Have you heard of spelt, teff, triticale, or couscous? These are some of the grains of ancient times. The most popular grain in

America is wheat, also found in graham flour, bulgur, cracked wheat, and wheat berries. Barley is used in soups and buckwheat, and can be called kasha. There is also millet, oats, rye, and the wonderful ancient Peruvian grain called Quinoa (Keenwah). Most of you are familiar with cornmeal and rice. It is entertaining to spend some time in the grain aisle and explore these unique, healthy grains. Many of the packages have the history of the grain on the label, plus suggested uses and cooking.

Memories of childhood include coming home from school and smelling the aroma of freshly baked bread just out of the oven. I can smell it now, can you? Some people have never stopped baking their own bread, and you can have a wonderful time trying diverse types of recipes. The good old-fashioned bakery is making a comeback, hooray! I hate to admit that my children went through a stage of preferring the soft, cotton-like white bread. There has been an increased demand for specialty and exotic type breads in recent years. This is partially due to the awareness that these breads are made with whole grain natural products. When using recipes or buying at the in-store bakery, read the label and make sure you are getting quality whole grains. The first items in the ingredient list should be unbleached enriched wheat flour, stone-ground or cracked wheat. The choices of bread products is, at times, overwhelming. You must be aware of the hidden fat in croissants, biscuits, muffins, puff pastry, coffee cakes, and doughnuts. Stay away from these products, except for special treats.

Let's go to the cereal aisle. They used to be called breakfast cereals, but now they are versatile and can be used for lunch, supper, or a snack anytime of day or night. You might find a lot of children shopping in this section, because of all the hype advertising for novelty cereals. The quality cereals probably could fit on one small shelf. When reading the label, make sure it says whole grain. Many packaged cereals have too much sugar, sodium, and preservatives. The nice thing about this group is that you can make a complete meal by adding fruit and milk. So simple, and so good for you. Back to our childhood memories again with cold cereal or a steaming bowl of hot cereal, such as oatmeal.

Another excellent bran is rice. Rice is a food staple for over half of the world. It can be used as a main dish, side dish, salad, in combination with other foods, and dessert. When shopping for rice, look for brown rice. This contains the most fiber. Even though the outer hull is removed, it still retains the bran layers. It has a distinctive nutty texture and flavor. Parboiled or converted white rice has been subjected to steam pressure, which pushes nutrients from the bran into the starchy center so they are lost when the rice is milled or the bran is removed. If you are now using white rice, gradually substitute brown rice in all of your recipes. Do not rinse white rice before cooking or you will wash away the enriched or added nutrients. Instant rice is the most refined, has the least amount of nutrients and fiber, and costs the most.

Pasta, pasta, pasta—all different in types, shapes, ingredients, and uses. It is another versatile carbohydrate, known for its energy-producing qualities. Twenty-five years ago, when my life was hectic with babies and preschoolers, I would need a fast, inexpensive meal, so good old macaroni and cheese was on the menu a lot. Now I realize how healthily I was treating my family. Look for the noodles and spaghetti products made from whole wheat, perhaps fortified with added protein, made from eggs and enriched with vitamins. You could serve pasta many times a week and never have boring meals. Pasta lends itself to light cooking, because you need very little protein to accompany it. One-half cup is a serving, and it is surprising how that amount satisfies your appetite.

Relearn the merits of the grain group. The bad press it received for years as being fattening is not true.

19

SNACKS/SWEETS

Everyone has his or her own idea of what a snack is. The dictionary defines it as a light meal between regular meals. Perhaps after the age of fifty, all of our meals should be designated as snacks, because we all should be eating lighter. Snacking is an area that has gained a negative reputation. Snacking had the connotation of being associated with teenage junk food. Old habits die hard, and for many older people snacking has been a lifelong hobby. Synonyms for snacking are nibbling, mini-meals, grazing, and piecing. All the food groups have popular snack foods and junk foods; our responsibility as we grow older is to make healthy choices. What we must do is adjust our thinking and be aware of a food's value instead of the empty calorie syndrome. Many people snack out of habit and it is often an emotional eating pattern to satisfy the chewing urge. A poll taken in several of my senior citizen nutrition classes indicated the majority of people did not snack because they were hungry, but for reasons of boredom and loneliness. However, recent analysis has revealed that snacking can be healthy! It can help people lose weight, lower cholesterol, and improve mental alertness. By having four to six mini-meals during the day, the assimilation of our food will be improved, resulting in a healthier digestive system.

Snacks: These can run the gamut from appetizers to desserts and everything in between. Let your imagination run wild, be creative, and you can come up with your own array of satisfying, unique snacks.

Hors d'oeuvres, appetizers, "before the meal" snacks, or antipasto can be beneficial if chosen wisely. This snack can be from any of the four food groups and can help appease our appetite so that we do not eat as much at our main meal.

Choose dips wisely. Make them light by using drained yogurt. Let yogurt rest in a cheesecloth or a sieve for 48 hours until it has a cream cheese-like consistency. Choose low-fat, low-salt crackers. Most snack crackers are high in fat. A good guideline is it should have less than 2–3 grams fat and less than 200 mg sodium per serving. A low-fat cheese has less than 2 grams of fat per ounce. The only cheese that is naturally this low is 1 percent low-fat cottage cheese. Modified "lite" cheeses are the other alternative. Use vegetables and fruit for dips and spreads instead of the high-fat potato chips and corn chips. Make your own chips by baking/broiling corn and flour tortillas.

The midmorning and midafternoon snacks really can help with that tired, down in the dumps feeling. Try some fruit with yogurt or a half piece of whole wheat bread, the perfect pick-me-up for that slump.

What about eating while you are watching television in the evening, or raiding the refrigerator in the middle of the night because of insomnia? Just leave all junk food at the store and concentrate on those nutrient-dense snacks. Try the popular rice cakes for a change of pace. Some people call popcorn the perfect snack food. It is high in fiber, low in calories, inexpensive, and convenient. Just make sure you use the new air-pop method and eat it plain or with lemon juice, herbs, and spices instead of salt and butter. Thirty cups of air-popped popcorn has the same amount of calories as one cup of peanuts. Chew it completely so you do not choke or break a tooth. Watch out for the unpopped kernels.

Sweets: One of the most sinful snack foods! And what is a meal without dessert? That is the thinking of many people in our generation. You never served a visitor just a cup of coffee; it always had to be accompanied by something sweet. What about sugar addicts and chocoholics?

I reviewed a 1975 book, *Sugar Blues*, by William Dufty. It is a controversial exposé on sugar. Every decade seems to have a nutrition crusade. If it isn't sugar, it is sodium, fat, cholesterol, vitamin C, calcium, and so on. I repeat, read those labels.

The amount of hidden sugar in foods we do not consider sweet is appalling. You can find sweets in every department of the grocery store. Soups and cereals are notorious for added sugar. Sugar can give you real highs and real lows. Added sugars provide extra calories but few nutrients.

Sugar means more than the white table sugar, but refers to all sweeteners, table sugar, brown sugar, honey, syrups, molasses, corn syrup, and dextrin. Also watch for words ending in ose like sucrose, fructose, maltose, and dextrose. Sugar is a simple carbohydrate. When reading the nutrition information on a product, it is difficult to determine how much is simple sugar and how much is complex carbohydrates. There are two things you can do to assess the amount of simple sugar: If a concentrated sugar appears on the list of ingredients as the first, second, or third ingredient, then it is likely to be quite high in simple sugar. For cereals, the bottom of the nutrition information panel has a chart listing grams of complex carbohydrates and grams of sucrose and other sugars. If the amount of sucrose is less than one half of the amount of complex carbohydrates then the product is low enough in simple sugars.

The number of artificial sweeteners can be perplexing. They are continuously under review by the Food and Drug Administration (FDA) and should be used sparingly.

It is better to satisfy your craving for something sweet by having occasional special treats. There are many light desserts on the market and many wholesome recipe books available. It is quite easy to modify dessert recipes and still have a delicious sweet treat. Some of these modifications also help to eliminate fat. Use only two thirds of the fat called for in a recipe, and two thirds of the sugar. To replace the moisture and sweetness, add fruit, such as mashed bananas or applesauce. Instead of unsweetened chocolate squares, use plain cocoa powder and one tablespoon of oil. Instead of a pastry crust, use a graham cracker crust with two tablespoons of fruit juice for a binder. There are many diet books available that feature creative desserts instead of the standard cookies, cakes, and pies. How about a piece of fruit? When you get attuned to thinking "sweet, but healthy and nutritious," a whole new world is waiting to be explored.

What are some general guidelines for snacking? Try to choose low-fat, low-sodium, low-sugar snacks. Think natural, simple foods. Read the labels. Plan and prepare your snacks so they are ready to eat when the urge hits. Modify the recipes with fewer calories, and sugar content. Do not be afraid to graze, have several mini-meals, and nibble. It is good for you if you do it the right way. If you detect some of your snacking is just a habit or unconscious eating, keep busy and find something else to occupy your time.

Remember, wise snacking starts with your menu planning and grocery list. If you follow these directives you will be able to "have your cake and eat it too!"

20

DENTAL HEALTH

Many times we think that education on certain health topics is meant for young people. Dental health is one of those topics. It is true, good dental hygiene should start at an early age. We have been told to brush our teeth after every meal, see the dentist regularly, use dental floss daily, and, of utmost significance, practice proper nutrition. Balance and moderation is again the key. Poor nutritional health can result in deficiencies and excesses that will affect the health of your mouth, tongue, gums, and teeth.

This key is a natural follow-up to the preceding Key, Snacks/ Sweets. The primary cause of tooth caries (tooth decay) is the consumption of sucrose-rich foods. Demineralization of the tooth enamel is caused by fermenting of simple carbohydrates (table sugar, corn syrup, honey), which produces lactic acid. It is a vicious cycle. Untreated dental caries can result in tooth loss, then these conditions prevent a person from chewing and eating adequate amounts of the right kinds of foods.

Complex carbohydrates (starches) also can be fermented by bacteria, but it takes a longer period of time. This type of food can become lodged between the teeth and gums. Meats and foods high in fiber, such as fresh fruits and vegetables, help clean the teeth of food particles and sugars during the chewing process. These foods promote saliva flow, which helps rinse the teeth of food, and the saliva also helps neutralize the acid. Fruits, vegetables, grains, and cereals help bolster the whole body, including the immune system, and this helps fight gum disease.

If you have been privileged to live in an area where fluoride was added to the water supply, your incidence of tooth decay is probably remarkably lower. This is a recent innovation in preventive medicine within the last 30 years, so my children have had fewer cavities than my husband and I. Many people now use fluoride rinses and toothpaste.

One beneficial but inexpensive thing we can do is to replace our toothbrush often. It is a breeding ground for bacteria, which can increase our chances of having tooth and gum problems. A soft bristle brush is gentler on the gums than a hard one.

Some difficulties that can be age-related are: canker sores, oral cancer, dry mouth, coated tongue, gum diseases, receding gums, and loss of teeth. Not every concern always can be prevented or treated by proper intake of nutrients, but "an ounce of prevention is worth a pound of cure." Most vitamins and minerals contribute to the health of the mouth, gums, and teeth. Regular dental checkups can detect the early stages of most of these conditions. Gum disease is the number one cause of older adults losing their natural teeth. Gingivitis can occur when the gums become inflamed and swollen because of plaque buildup. A more serious periodontal problem is the decay of the bone tissue that supports the teeth. The flow of saliva decreases with age (dry mouth), which can be caused by vitamin deficiencies, illness, and medications. Dry mouth can cause tooth decay, and the intake of proper nutrition can then be difficult. Drink plenty of water with meals to help prevent dry mouth, or try using artificial saliva and effective mouth rinses, especially formulated to inhibit the dry mouth condition. The enamel of the teeth has a tendency to darken with age. There are now techniques available to whiten and brighten the enamel.

The teeth have other functions besides helping grind, chew, cut, tear, and crush our food. They aid in the production of sounds and help with clear speech. They also influence the shape and appearance of the face, which can affect your feeling of self-worth and your emotional health.

If there is a problem with chewing, it is advantageous to grind or chop fruits, vegetables, and meats. You can prepare your food in soups, stews, and casseroles. If you rely entirely. on a soft food diet, your teeth could deteriorate even more and you will not be exercising your facial and jaw muscles. Avoid acidic and spicy foods and extremely hot or cold food. People with arthritis and strokes need to take extra care in making sure they do not neglect proper care of their teeth, even though with impaired physical dexterity it may be difficult to eat and brush their teeth.

Having false teeth, dentures, or implants need not be an obstacle. Investing in quality, well-fitting dentures is imperative. Do not settle for an okay fit. They take time to adjust to, and daily oral hygiene is just as important.

As long as we are in the supermarket, go to the health care shelves and get a good toothbrush, some dental floss, toothpaste, and mouthwash, *smile* and show off those pearly whites!

21

CONDIMENTS/SPREADS

Condiments are used to enhance the flavor of food, such as a seasoning or relish, sauces, and toppings. They can be appetizers, garnishes, side dishes, snacks, main courses, salads, desserts, small amounts added to other foods, or garnish for foods. Condiments can be in all your menus: breakfast, lunch, and dinner. They can add variety and nutrition to your meals. Some words that come to mind when we think of condiments are: sour, bitter, sweet, strong, pungent, hot mild, tangy, and savory. This Key will require us to visit several sections of the store, but can't you just visualize the aisle containing all condiments? Let's explore pickles, peppers, olives, ketchups, barbecue sauces, mustards, dressings, mayonnaises, soy, Worcestershire, plus the jams, jellies, and sweets in this category.

It is imperative that you get in the habit of studying labels. At times you feel like you have to have a degree in chemistry to understand the contents of foods. Sometimes the additives can be frightening, but the main points to recall are the amounts of fat, sodium, and sugar that they contain.

If we were to go back to the good old days and make ketchup, pickles, preserves, jellies, and so on from "scratch," we would not have to have warnings about reading labels. Do you recall your grandmother or mother making pickles at home or getting them from a big barrel at the local grocery store? What a wonderful experience! I can almost smell and taste the freshness today. Would you believe, I now am using my pickle crocks for flower pots! Ah, memories.

Back to the supermarket. We are very fortunate to have a wonderful selection of condiments in all food groups and for all purposes. We need to use our creativity and discover the many ways we can incorporate them into our daily food plans. Some of them do not have a lot of food value, so you must choose them wisely.

Here are a few practical suggestions for the many condiments on the shelf, and hopefully some innovative ideas to spark your own inventiveness. Instead of using highly pickled products, which usually are very high in sodium, use fresh cut vegetables, such as cucumbers, radishes, carrots, celery, and onions. Remember, olives are high in fat and a few go a long way. You must watch the sodium content in soy sauces, mustards, and ketchups. There is a "lite" variety of soy sauce and a large variety of mustards. Make your own chutney-type relish from various fruits and spices. Be cognizant of the "low-oil" and "no-oil" salad dressings and mayonnaise-type salad dressings. Dilute or make your own dressings from yogurt, dried skim milk, and tofu. Instead of high-fat sauces and gravies, try spicy salsa, picante, or taco sauce to add flavor. Salsa or picante sauce is a fabulous potato topper instead of butter or sour cream.

For sweet toppings on toast and desserts, use pureed fresh fruit or apple butter. There are many commercially made sugar-free jams and jellies on the shelves, but perhaps you prefer to make your own. It's a simple procedure.

So, hopefully, this will help you discover the old and new world of condiments.

22

CANNED/FROZEN

Another product that has gone from a good reputation to a bad one and now back to a good one is canned goods. When most of the canned goods were actually in glass jars prepared right in our kitchens, we were assured of fresh-from-the-garden food and few added preservatives. With the invention of the lead can for preserving food, we were unaware of the possible toxicity that the use of those cans provided us. Now when we refer to tin cans, it usually means safe, nontoxic steel. Former canning processes produced overprocessed fruits and vegetables of poor quality, lacking in vitamins and minerals, and high in sodium.

Today's canned goods offer convenience, easy storage, a long shelf life, good nutrition, and sometimes are less expense than fresh or frozen. They save much food preparation time and are convenient to have on our storage shelf or pantry. It is important to understand the labeling to make sure they are not too high in sodium (not more than 200 mg per serving) and sugar. Pure vegetables and fruits are negligible in fat content, but beware of sodium, sugars, plus fat in canned soups. Make sure you look for reduced-sodium or no-salt-added versions. New products constantly are being added to this category.

When selecting canned fruits, look for fruits packed in juice or water rather than heavy syrup, so you can cut down on sugar in your diet. Notice the difference in the names on the labels of fruit juices. There is a difference in content between pure fruit juices, nectars, juice cocktails, punches, and juice drinks that contain little fruit juice.

Vegetables and soups can be added to other ingredients to make tasty stews and casseroles. Be careful when purchasing fish products, such as tuna, and choose water packed over the oil. Look for generic canned goods; often the only distinction between the name brands and generic is the color, shape, and texture, and generic goods usually are less expensive.

Put on your mittens, scarf, and hat and let's go to the frozen food section. The selection here has grown tremendously in both quality and quantity in recent years. The quality of frozen vegetables often is better than fresh because there is less handling involved. The vegetables are harvested and frozen at their peak of ripeness. They also don't require salt for preservation as in canned goods. The simpler the product, the less fat, sodium, sugar, and calories, and the lower the price. When you start adding batters, breadings, sauces, and deep-fat frying to foods, you add fat, sodium, and a higher price. Some people prefer frozen vegetables over canned. When cooking for one or two, you can buy the jumbo or family size, which is more economical and enables you to use only what you need. Do not overlook the good fruit selection with many varieties of berries, peaches, and mixed fruit.

At the other end of the scale are complete gourmet dinners. There is no comparison between the old TV dinners of the 1950s and the ones available today. Some of the advertising is misleading and it becomes your responsibility to read the labels. The variety of "light meals" can be confusing; some are low in calories and fat, but all could do a better job at reducing the sodium content. A simple rule is if a frozen entrée has 10 grams of fat or less, it usually is under 30 percent fat. Another reminder: the total fat intake on a daily basis should be under that percentage.

For the empty nester, retired people, working couples, and people living alone, the potpourri in the frozen food section is captivating. This includes low-calorie desserts in individual servings so you won't be tempted to overindulge.

By all means explore the idea of cooking larger quantities of food at home and then making your own frozen dinners. There still is nothing on the market that beats home cooking. Use your freezer at home for your mini frozen food section of the supermarket. It is also a good idea to store other foodstuffs, such as coffee and popcorn, in the freezer for freshness and a longer shelf life. Always wrap the food properly and freeze it fast. To defrost, take it from the freezer and let it thaw gradually in the refrigerator. Don't thaw at room temperature. For rapid defrosting, you may follow the instructions to your micro-wave.

Thank goodness we have come a long way from the days when our ancestors preserved food by hanging the food outside and drying it!

23

CONVENIENCE FOODS/ MICROWAVING

According to the dictionary, "convenience" means anything that saves work, is handy, and is easy to do. As we grow older and wiser, we want more and more areas of our life to be just that. Hopefully you will find that many of these Keys will make general nutrition, planning, shopping, cooking, and eating more convenient in your later years of life.

The previous two Keys also could be titled convenience foods, for we find many handy, easy-to-fix foods in the canned goods aisles and in the frozen food sections. This leaves the dry, boxed, and packaged foods, another area of advancement in preservation techniques. Packaging in plastic was not known when our grandmothers, mothers, and even we shopped. Everything was purchased in bulk, and you weighed and measured the amount you wanted. Talk about having come a long way! Dry packaged food now extends from very simple, pure food, such as the great variety of pastas, to the elaborate gourmet dinners, all in one convenient box. Take your time browsing in this aisle and see how many different boxed foodstuffs there are. I think you will be surprised. They are assembled in a variety of different ways, and all are preserved a little differently. Some are a much healthier version than years ago, whereas others are still too high in preservatives, sodium, fat, and sugar.

It was my job on the farm when I was raised to collect the wood for the cookstove. From that stove came wonderful meals and from the oven, delicious baked goods. It is truly amazing what great food we produced with such modest equipment.

77

It is hard to believe that microwave cooking has been around for almost 50 years. Today, many kitchens have a microwave oven; it is estimated over 80 percent of American households have one. It is called an oven because it looks more like an oven, but can do many of the jobs of the top-of-the-range stove, without the mess, in less time, and with less attention and easier cleanup. A baked potato, which takes about 45 minutes in a conventional oven, is done in only eight minutes in a microwave oven, saving time and energy. One of the amazing characteristics of microwave energy is that it heats the food, not the utensil. Do not warm a baby bottle when babysitting grandchildren, as the milk can be a lot hotter than you think.

Because microwaving cooks very fast, it is very easy to overcook foods. The food cooks completely, even though external appearances would suggest that the product is not cooked completely. Foods usually taste the same, but can look different. They will not brown or crust over. We are accustomed in conventional cooking to aesthetically pleasing cuisine, as well as a good flavor.

It is important to get a good instructional cookbook and to follow the exact directions and procedures. There are microwave cooking classes that can be of value. Many times we end up using the microwave as an expensive way to make a cup of coffee or heat up leftovers. You can eat out of the same bowl you cooked in too. Regular recipes can be adapted to microwaves, but to take the guesswork out of it, I prefer using a recipe that already has been converted to that type of cooking.

Many foods have improved flavor and quality with this type of cooking. Some of these foods are vegetables, potatoes, eggs, and fish. Other foods are casseroles, meats, and desserts. It is perfect for leftovers, reheating a meal, and defrosting. It is an efficient way to cook for one or two people, and many times older people find they are eating healthier because they have purchased a microwave. You also can combine stove-top cooking, a conventional oven, and microwaving with many recipes. Because added fat is not required, it is a low-fat cooking method. Fat can be added for flavor, but is not essential in microwaving. Another advantage is that fruits and vegetables retain many of the vitamins and minerals because less liquid is used in their cooking.

Microwaving saves time and money for small quantities of food, however, it is not always as economical for cooking larger portions.

The USDA has been concerned about the consumer recognizing the importance of using the microwave safely. Here are some tips on utensils and materials to use for defrosting, warming, and cooking foods safely. Use plain white paper goods, never brown grocery bags. Waxed paper is safe, as well as oven cooking bags. Do not let plastic wrap touch foods. Do not reuse containers provided with microwave convenience products. They have been designed for onetime use with that specific food only. Use only those containers and products that have been approved for microwave use. Containers that have not been approved for microwaving and high heat could cause chemicals to transfer into the food.

If you use the microwave to defrost food, finish cooking it immediately. Prior to thawing, remove the store wrapping.

When warming precooked foods, cover with a glass lid, waxed paper, or microwave-safe plastic. The internal temperature should be 160° F, and food should be very hot to the touch and steaming before it is served.

Before cooking, arrange food uniformly in a covered dish. Follow exact directions; some items are cooked at 50 percent power for longer periods of time. Move and rotate the food several times during cooking. Read all directions carefully and follow them exactly. It is better to be safe than sorry.

We deserve to enjoy this time of life, and if we use convenience foods and the convenience of a microwave, we will have more time for other pleasurable pursuits.

24

SALT/HERBS/SPICES

Another area that you will take time strolling in is the salt, herb, and spice section. What an array of wonderful products and aromas! Salt has a long history dating back thousands of years. It is one of the earliest known preservatives, because it has the ability to draw water out of food, thus reducing the incidence of harmful bacteria. Salt was so precious that wars were fought over the salt deposits. Besides being a preservative, salt acts as a flavor enhancer and helps to maintain freshness and texture.

The word *salt* or sodium chloride is used interchangeably, but table salt is actually 40 percent sodium and 60 percent chloride. Sodium is an important mineral in the body and is useful to regulate the fluid balance. It helps maintain normal blood pressure and volume, and attracts water into the blood vessels. Excessive salt in the diet is linked with high blood pressure, or hypertension. Excess sodium can result in water retention, which may put a strain on the blood vessels, heart, and kidneys.

It is difficult to dictate the desired intake of salt, because it depends on climate, physical activity, age, and general overall health. About one third of the salt we consume is from the processed food we eat, one third is what we add during cooking or eating, and one third occurs naturally in foods. The American Heart Association recommends limiting your daily sodium intake to 3,000 milligrams per day. How can we judge that amount? A teaspoon of salt contains 2,000 milligrams of sodium. Most American diets get an excess of salt on a daily basis. It is best to remove the saltshaker from the table. Moderation is the key word.

What are some tips for controlling the amount of sodium in your diet? Fresh fruits and vegetables, fresh meats and poultry, and grains are naturally low in sodium. Most cheeses, processed lunch meats, baked goods, dry cereals, and canned soups are high in sodium. Label reading is essential. Also, be aware of the amount of salt you add when you are cooking or at the table when you are eating. Another tip is to put tape over half of the holes in the saltshaker. Be on the lookout for low-salt, low-sodium, and sodium-reduced products. Try to gradually wean yourself from excessive salt intake. This taste is acquired from childhood and it takes time to adjust to the authentic taste of foods. Sparingly use salty foods like nuts, potato chips, soy sauce, and condiments, such as mustard and pickle relish. Rinse canned foods, which usually contain a large quantity of salt.

Is it okay to use the salt substitute products? Your body has a delicate balance of sodium and potassium working together. These products have a tendency to be high in potassium. All of the products contain a varying amount of sodium. Again, read those labels. It is best to create your own salt substitute from herbs and spices, or use lemon juice for seasoning.

Though research and studies are still inconclusive, most evidence shows that the older we get the more prevalent is high blood pressure, thus leading to other complications and diseases. So, if you can't cut out salt, at least cut down.

Other terms that can be confusing are herbs and spices. Yes, there is a difference. An *herb* is a part of a plant, usually leafy, that grows in temperate zones. *Spices* are a part of a plant grown in tropical regions, and include stems, roots, flowers, bark, buds, and seeds. They are available fresh, frozen, or dried, and come either whole or ground. They are used to enhance flavor and add a spark and zest to many foods in all of the food groups. Americans are using more spices than ever. This is due to the challenge to reduce the amount of salt used and also the burgeoning interest in ethnic cooking.

Thank goodness the herbs and spices are conveniently alphabetized; that is how I keep them in my own spice shelf. The label usually tells what each is to be used for. Herbs and spices should be stored in dark, airtight containers. In the produce section you will see a variety of fresh herbs to choose from. The idea of starting an herb garden is on my future hobby list. The garden can be either outdoors or indoors, in a spot where it will get morning or afternoon sun, not too much water, and with room to expand. Remember, we are discussing culinary herbs in this Key, not the ones advocated for medicinal purposes.

Each herb and spice has a character, smell, and taste all of its own. A small amount usually goes a long way. You do not want to overpower the food, just improve the flavor. Periodically, it is a good idea to replace your herbs and spices, especially the ones you use infrequently. Often you can buy small quantities from a health food store to refill your jars, and the saving is substantial. Some of the common herbs to try are mint, parsley, chervil, sage, rosemary, thyme, and basil. In the interesting world of spices are allspice (a blend of cinnamon, nutmeg, and cloves), cayenne, chili powder, curry, and ginger.

It is a challenge to learn new and different ways of using the herbs and spices available to us for more creative and healthy seasoning of our favorite foods.

25

WATER

Of all of the nutrients for total nutrition, water is number one! We can survive a much longer time without food than we can without water. It ranks second to air as being essential for survival. Water serves many purposes for all of our body processes. It aids all the processes of digestion and is important to our circulatory and excretory systems. Water carries waste out of the body and it helps to regulate body temperature. It lubricates and cushions joints, and softens the skin. It is ironic that the majority of our cells, blood, brain, and some of our bones are made up of water and the largest percentage of most foods is also water, particularly fruits and vegetables.

As we age, there are other important factors associated with adequate intake of fluids. Water is lost by the process of elimination, through breathing, and in perspiration. It is mandatory that we make a conscientious effort to replace the water lost each day. For some people this comes easily, but for many of us this becomes a chore. Many older people have an impaired sense of thirst and don't seek water even when it is physically needed and easily available. Dehydration is the most common cause of a brief period of confusion. One of the major reasons there are more bladder infections with older people is because of dehydration. Drinking plenty of water dilutes the concentration of bacteria in the urine and encourages urination so the bacteria are expelled. Drinking plenty of fluids also helps soften stools, resulting in fewer episodes of constipation. Drinking water also can deter the formation of kidney stones.

A very general rule is to consume at least eight 8-ounce glasses of water a day. Some variables are general health status, the medications you take, the amount of exercise you get, and the climate you live in, plus other individual factors. Do not wait until you are thirsty to drink water, but get in the habit of drinking periodically all day long. I carry with me a container with a straw; I might be one of those who does not drink enough. Some people have a pitcher and glass handy on their kitchen counter. How about putting eight pennies in a pocket on your right-hand side. Every time you drink a glass of water, put a penny in the left-hand pocket. When all pennies are in the left-hand pocket you did well! If you are like a camel and prefer to go without drinking water, you should be aware that you can meet some of your fluid needs from other foods and beverages (milk, juice, jello, pudding, herb teas, and soups). Devise an individual method for yourself to assure that your body is getting enough of this number one nutrient every day.

After reading some of the literature about the dangers lurking in some water systems, perhaps you are wondering why I recommend drinking water at all. The Federal Safe Drinking Water Act was enacted in 1974 and revised in 1986. Some experts believe the safety of our drinking water is one of the most important issues of the 90s. The public and private water supplies are regulated much more closely than they were years ago. Of course, our water supplies are coming in contact with more pollutants today than ever before. The contaminants and toxins in many water supplies measure in the hundreds. To understand the complexity of the problems, you can send for free EPA pamphlets, "Is Your Drinking Water Safe?" and "Buying a Water Treatment Unit." Call the EPA's Safe Drinking Water Hotline: (800) 426-4791, for these pamphlets or for answers to any other question or concerns you may have.

One of the biggest threats is the amount of lead found in our water. It not only affects infants and children, but some researchers believe it can worsen high blood pressure in adults. You can do something about the drinking water in your own home even though you cannot see, smell, or taste lead. Before using water for drinking or cooking, "flush" the cold water faucet by allowing the water to run until you can feel that the

84

water has become as cold as it will get. This is especially important if it has been in contact with your home's plumbing for more than six hours without running. Never cook with or consume water from the hot water tap. Hot water dissolves more lead more quickly than cold water. Also, contact your supplier, such as your city water department, and find out as much as you can about where the water supply originates, the location of treatment facilities, water pipes and mains, and so on.

So, is it better to drink bottled water? Sorry, this is another gray area in nutrition with no standard answer. Bottled water is over a $2 billion industry and the number of people of all ages who buy and use bottled water is growing steadily year after year. According to a poll by the International Bottled Water Association, people purchase bottled water for various reasons. The primary reason is taste, and they feel it is cleaner, purer, and healthier.

The Food and Drug Administration (FDA) has classified bottled water as a food. Many of the harmful substances have been removed from many of the bottled waters. It is a controversial and confusing topic. To get more information on this subject, write the International Bottled Water Association, 113 N. Henry Street, Alexandria, Virginia 22314, or call you local bottled water company. If you have any questions on water safety, call the Environmental Protection Agency (EPA) at 1-800-428-4791.

No matter what form of water you choose to achieve your goal of drinking eight glasses a day, just do it. H_2O is a vital nutrient that often is neglected.

26

OTHER BEVERAGES

If you cannot drink eight glasses of water a day, consider other beverages, such as herbal teas, fruit juices, and soft drinks. Coffee and tea are dehydrators, so they don't satisfy your need for water. Here's another aisle of the supermarket in which to take your time and have fun shopping, but you can find more confusion. During the last 30 years, the effects of coffee have been researched, studied, refuted, given the okay, given negative press, then said it is all right to drink. I could just stop writing this Key on coffee right now and say stay tuned for the next saga, probably in tomorrow's newspaper. We are getting so many mixed messages on this subject. Even the experts cannot agree.

I can remember sneaking over to the neighbor's house when I was about twelve to have a cup of coffee, with loads of cream and sugar. My parents would not allow me to drink it at home. Of course, we think nothing of permitting children to indulge in other caffeine-containing substances, such as soda pop and chocolate. Can you remember your first encounter with the "big people's" drink? It is the second most popular beverage after water.

Caffeine is considered the most widely used psychoactive drug in America. It acts directly on the central nervous system to stimulate the release of brain chemicals. The body absorbs caffeine quickly, and it takes days to completely remove all of it from the body. Caffeine is addictive and can cause physical dependency. Caffeine also is found in many over-the-counter drugs, so read those labels.

The list of negative claims of consuming coffee is extensive: it increases the heart rate, elevates blood pressure, intensifies the production of stomach acid, is thought to contribute to some forms of cancer, higher cholesterol levels, and birth defects. Additionally, it is associated with a whole gamut of symptoms: nervousness, insomnia, daytime fatigue, dry mouth, lightheadedness, racing or skipping heartbeat, tremors or shaking, ulcers, heartburn, diarrhea, constipation, and frequent urination. Do you really want it? Although coffee is a liquid, you can't count it as some of your daily fluid because it dehydrates you. Wow, I wonder if just walking down the coffee aisle at the supermarket could be dangerous to one's health!

Are there any positives? Caffeine keeps you mentally alert, improves athletic performance, can provide relief to some asthma sufferers, and sometimes helps with weight loss. Again, the research is not proof positive.

Another Key could be written on the good and bad factors related to drinking decaffeinated coffee. Decaffeinated without using chemicals seems to be a better alternative as we get older. Read the label, and choose a coffee that has been naturally decaffeinated using pure water and oil from the coffee bean. Stay away from coffee decaffeinated with formaldehyde. So, why take a chance, why not cut it out, or at least cut down to a moderate amount. An arbitrary figure is 200 milligrams of caffeine per day, or about two 6-ounce cups of coffee.

Coming from German and English ancestry, I grew up appreciating the sociability of coffee and tea. To me tea is tranquilizing, refreshing, secure, relaxing, recharging, and even medicinal. It has quite an amazing history—even battles were fought over it. It probably originated in China, which is still the biggest producer, but India also exports a great deal of tea. Although tea does have caffeine in it, it is not as concentrated as in coffee. I find no difference in the taste or quality of decaffeinated tea. Because of the health conscious society we live in, herbal teas have gained in esteem. There is an extensive variety to choose from, such as orange blossom, rosehip, cinnamon, raspberry, chamomile, lemon, mint, and so on. Be sure that you are not allergic to any of the herbs used in these teas.

Brewing a proper cup of tea is an art. This is a cherished learning experience from my English mother. Start with quality loose tea or a tea bag. Use cool water and bring it to a boil, remove immediately to retain the most oxygen. Warm the teapot or cup with some of the hot water. Pour the boiling water over the tea, cover, and let it brew or infuse for about five minutes. Teas are wonderful hot or cold. Enjoy!

Walking down the soft drink, soda pop, or pop aisle is another adventure. What a selection! When a guest comes to our house, we not only have to name off several brands, but also, ask if you want regular with caffeine, regular without caffeine, diet with caffeine, or diet and caffeine-free. Decision making!

I guess a health drink is any drink that is considered to be good for you. The manufacturers of so called "health drinks" are jumping on the health-craze bandwagon and furnishing consumers with many types of drinks. They do add to your grocery bill. They are caffeine-free, fat-free, sugar-free, and so on. Some of them are indeed good for you and it is fun to try new products, but read those labels.

So, to settle all of these controversial comments, how about a glass of 100 percent (no sugar added) orange, grapefruit, apple, or grape juice?

27

BOWEL PROBLEMS

One of the common concerns of older adults is bowel problems. We will discuss them only briefly; if any of these conditions exist, you should consult your health care provider to find out if the problem is serious. As we grow older, the main worry seems to be constipation. *Constipation* is a decrease of bowel movements, accompanied by difficult or prolonged passage of stools. It also can refer to hardness of a stool and the feeling of incomplete evacuation. Many times older people are overly concerned with this problem and it becomes an obsession with them.

What is meant by "regularity" varies from individual to individual. The notion that we must have one bowel movement a day is erroneous. It can be "normal" to have several a day or to have just a few a week.

There are many reasons why constipation is so prevalent among older people. Our whole digestive system is not as efficient, a diet may be lacking in fiber, we may be drinking too few liquids, and there may be a lack of interest in eating. Other causes of constipation are an accident, illness, lack of exercise, use of certain drugs and prescriptions and misuse of laxatives.

Many people feel that laxatives are helpful for constipation, when in fact extended use usually is not necessary and often can be habit-forming. If laxatives are used long enough, you can become dependent on them. The best remedy for constipation is to eat a well-balanced diet high in fiber foods, such as whole grain bread and cereals, and fresh fruits and vegetables. Try to eat slowly, exercise regularly, and limit or avoid caffeine and alcohol.

Constipation can cause hemorrhoids to develop because of pressure on the rectal veins. This weakens and enlarges the veins and they become inflamed and bleed. Treatment usually is suppositories and warm baths, or for extreme cases surgery sometimes is necessary.

Diarrhea in someone over fifty can have several causes, such as an infection, illness, medications, overuse of laxatives, or too many bowel-loosening foods, such as prunes and fruit juices. Treatment should be advised by your doctor. It doesn't seem rational, but when you have diarrhea, it is important to drink plenty of liquids to replace the lost fluids. A simple tip to help relieve diarrhea is the BRAT diet: bananas, rice, applesauce, and tapioca.

Diverticulosis can be caused from constipation and is common in older people. This is a condition where small sacs called diverticuli form on the wall of the large intestine, resulting in pain and inflammation. Prevention of diverticulosis includes a high-fiber diet and plenty of liquids. If you have an inflamed stage called divertic*ulitis*, avoid fiber and consume a "soft diet" for a day or two to let your intestines rest. A soft diet may be white bread sandwiches, canned fruit, broth soups, saltines and graham crackers, jello and pudding. Gradually reintroduce fiber back into your diet to prevent another flare-up. At all times avoid nuts, seeds, chunky peanut butter, coconut, popcorn, dried peas and beans, and raw broccoli.

Be aware of a sudden change in bowel habits, pains, cramps, sudden weight loss, black stools. Make sure you see your doctor promptly to prevent additional difficulties from occurring.

28

DIFFICULTIES/PRECAUTIONS
WHEN EATING

It may seem like we have jumped from the supermarket to the doctor's office, emergency room, or local health care facility. But, we must be realistic in our thinking; some eating difficulties could happen to us at age fifty or ninety. Many of us at one time or another have experienced eating difficulties, resulting primarily from sore mouths, chewing improperly, swallowing, and occasional choking episodes.

I can recall the fear I had feeding my children when they were babies. The apprehension was that they would not chew and swallow their food properly and would choke. The same anxiety can return with us or someone we know. The difficulties with sore and dry mouth and chewing usually are related to dental health (see Key 20).

Think about the ability to swallow your food if you did not have adequate moisture in your mouth. It would be very difficult, practically impossible. *Swallowing disorders* (dysphagias) become more common the older we get. Another process we take for granted is the body's production of saliva. With advancing age the amount of saliva decreases, making it more and more difficult to swallow correctly. If you notice a *dry mouth* (xerostomia) and a decrease in the flow of saliva, have a medical evaluation, as it could be due to medications or an underlying disease.

A *hiatal hernia* also can make eating unpleasant and can cause indigestion. This is a condition where a valve that separates the esophagus from the stomach fails to close and stomach acids splash up into the esophagus or throat and cause a burning sensation. This is common after middle age and only periodically causes problems. Treatment of hiatal hernia in-

91

cludes weight loss and avoidance of certain foods that actually relax the valve and cause it to remain open. These foods are tomatoes, fatty foods, spicy foods, peppermint or spearmint, alcohol, caffeine, hot cocoa, chocolate, and nicotine from cigarettes. Additionally it is important not to lie down for at least one hour after eating. Some people have trouble with swallowing liquids because they pool-up in the throat and can leak down into the lungs. There are commercial products available to thicken liquids for easier swallowing. Contact a dietitian or speech pathologist at your local hospital for an evaluation and more tips.

What can we do to prevent swallowing and choking complications? While eating, make sure you are sitting in a comfortable, upright position. Good posture is very important when eating, with the head upright or slightly tilted forward. This helps gravity assist in keeping the food forward in the mouth and prevents it from going into the throat before it is properly chewed. Make sure you take your time, taking small bites, and chewing it thoroughly before initiating the swallowing action.

Chances are that all of you can relate some frightening experiences when you have witnessed someone choking on food. My husband has been in the situation twice of saving someone's life by administering the *Heimlich maneuver*. Everyone, especially the over fifty crowd, should be proficient in administering the Heimlich maneuver. If someone is conscious and cannot breathe, cough, or speak, that is your clue to ask if he or she is choking. If the person can't answer, begin immediately. Stand behind the victim and put your arms around his waist. Make a fist with one hand and place your fist (thumbs in) against the person's stomach, just above the navel. Place your hands well below the rib cage. Grasp your fist with your other hand and press into the stomach with a quick upward thrust. Repeat the thrust until the lodged food particle is free. This Heimlich maneuver (abdominal thrust) could injure someone, so do not practice on people, but be knowledgeable and prepared to use it when indicated. This is just a short explanation of the procedure and never should be attempted without taking a class from a professionally trained person.

If the victim is unconscious, you will have to clear the mouth and attempt CPR (cardiopulmonary resuscitation). As I recommended in *Keys to Fitness Over Fifty,* sign up for a first aid and CPR class. The life you save could be that of someone you love.

They now have exercises for everything and "Prevention is worth a pound of cure." If you are worried that you might have *dysphagia* (a problem with normal transfer of your food from the mouth, pharynx, esophagus, to the stomach) try this eating exercise. Open your mouth wide several times. Move your tongue from side to side and in and out of your mouth. Open your mouth, close it, and swallow. Press your lips together and swallow. This will not harm you and could contribute to a more enjoyable eating experience by more efficient swallowing.

Some tips on cooking and eating that could help with sore mouth and chewing and swallowing difficulties are to add low-fat, low-sodium gravies and sauces to foods. Cook foods a longer period so they are tender, and use moist heat, such as braising, sautéing, and boiling for cooking. Chop or grate vegetables and fruit, or choose cooked or canned vegetables and fruit. Many foods are naturally soft and moist; smother your pancake in applesauce, make mashed potatoes extra soft by adding skim milk. Try whipped gelatin, hot cereal, custards, scrambled eggs, or egg and tuna salads. Thin liquids are most risky for swallowing difficulties. Many dysphagias benefit from a sauce that helps the food stay in a cohesive mass as you swallow it. There are professional speech pathologists who specialize in swallowing difficulties.

29

KITCHEN ORGANIZATION/ SAFETY

We finally have arrived home from the grocery store with our arms full of groceries. Grocery shopping can be a good physical fitness exercise; those aisles are long and the grocery cart gets unwieldy. We want to emphasize safety and convenience when it comes to organizing our kitchen as we get older. My husband still has a difficult time adjusting to the fact that I do not need to spend six hours a day in the kitchen as I did when we had a busy growing family. We can have healthier meals by cooking plain and simple fare. Remember, this book is for women and men; many men are enjoying food shopping and cooking at this stage of life, and are concerned about eating healthier.

The Kitchen: the heart of the home. Over the lifetime of most people, we probably spend more time in the kitchen than any other room in our home, not just in preparing and cooking meals, but in communicating and socializing. Think back to your grandparents' and parents' kitchens. There are many fond memories of that significant room in every home.

"Safety first," should be everyone's motto throughout life, but becomes critical the older we get. There are numerous hazards in our kitchens. Home accidents, especially falls, are one of the leading causes of injury and death. In your kitchen, examine the throw rugs and mats, the range area, electrical cords, lighting, step stools, and the telephone area.

Evaluate the safeness of the above mentioned areas and equipment. Consider throwing those throw rugs away. The major cause of tripping and falling is mats and rugs. You may trip on the edges and they also have a tendency to slide. If you must use scatter rugs, make sure they have slip-resistant backing.

The incidence of fires in the range area can be a worry. Are towels, curtains, and other things that might catch fire located away from the range? Store flammable and combustible items away from the range and oven.

Extension cords and appliance cords should be located away from the sink and range areas. Make sure to replace frayed or cracked cords. Do not overload extension cords. Better yet, try to have appliances close to an outlet so you do not have to use an extension cord. Do have smoke detectors that are in good working order.

Make sure there is adequate lighting over the stove, sink, and countertop work areas, especially where food is sliced or cut. Make sure that the bulbs you use are the right type and wattage for the light fixtures.

If you must use a step stool, make sure it is stable and in good repair. Use a step stool with a handrail that you can hold onto while standing on it. A better plan is to place everything in your kitchen within a convenient reach so you do not need a step stool.

Your best friend can be your telephone. Do you have access to a telephone if you fall (or experience some other emergency that prevents you from standing and reaching a wall phone)? Be sure to post emergency numbers on or near the telephone and have at least one telephone located where it would be accessible in the event of an accident.

An excellent book put out by the U.S. Consumer Product Safety Commission in Washington, D.C., *Safety For Older Consumers,* goes into detail on home safety, with a checklist for every area of your home. Call 1-800-638-2772 for your free copy. It could be the most important telephone call you ever make.

The household equipment classes I took in college were not always practical when it came to kitchen arrangement. How you organize your kitchen is a very personal matter; no two kitchens are arranged exactly the same. We do get in a rut and feel that we do not need to make any changes. But, what was good 30, 40, or 50 years ago may not be the best for you today. A review of some general kitchen guidelines may assist you in assessing whether some adjustments or modifications are necessary.

A kitchen usually is divided into three or four work centers: the mixing or preparation center, cooking center, sink center, and refrigerator center. The pantry center will be discussed in the next Key.

We probably spend more time in the preparation center than any other space in the kitchen. You want your ingredients and utensils stored efficiently. The cooking and stove center should be adjacent to the preparation center. Store pots and pans near the stove or in the stove drawer. The sink center should be handy to the cooking center and the eating area. A wastebasket and all dishwashing supplies are convenient if stored under the sink area. Near the refrigerator area should be storage for leftovers, and counter space to take food in and out of the refrigerator. Walk around your kitchen and write down areas where you might make some changes for the purpose of safety and convenience. If you do not have a desk center, adapt a space for cookbooks, menu planning, coupon files, calendars, a bulletin board, and so on.

Gadgets, gadgets. How many junk drawers do you have in your kitchen? Some synonyms for gadgets are contraptions, devices, gimmicks, doodads, and thingamajigs. You should take stock of your gadgets as you do your wardrobe. Ask yourself these questions. Do I need this? Do I use this? Does it work? Do I have more than one? Perhaps you should contemplate putting it away, giving it away, or throwing it away. You be the final judge. But do make some changes in your kitchen. Our needs today are different from when we were in our twenties, thirties, and forties. But, the kitchen still is the heart and soul of our homes.

30

FOOD SAFETY AND STORAGE

From the earliest attempts of cavemen, mankind has struggled to find ways to dry, smoke, salt, and generally preserve food for consumption at a later time. It was a very overwhelming task compared to modern-day food preservation. Yet today, with all of our modern technology, the safekeeping of food has become an enormous health problem. The incidence of food-borne illnesses is on the rise.

Even though we ourselves may have been handling, storing, and cooking food for years, it is advantageous for us to review the safety rules. At times, anyone might become careless.

The senses are important in many areas of our lives, but when it comes to food poisoning, many times we cannot see, smell, or taste the culprits. There is a difference between the organisms that cause food to spoil and the ones that cause food-borne illnesses. Botulism, salmonella, staph, and perfringens are the four main food poisoners, plus others.

Make the grocery store your last stop when running errands. When shopping, it is advisable to put last in your shopping cart the perishable items, such as meats, poultry, fish, milk products, and fresh foods. When you return home, immediately put away the foods that need to be refrigerated or frozen. Read the "sell by" and "use by" dates printed on many products; do not buy or use anything that is outdated.

Most of the problems can be prevented or controlled in your kitchen by adhering to three simple rules: (1) keep your kitchen clean, including your hands; (2) always use hot, soapy water and clean dish cloths; and (3) keeping cold foods cold (below 40° F) and hot foods hot (above 140° F).

Cross contamination is another concern. Always wash hands, utensils, countertops, and dishes with hot soapy water after they have been in contact with raw meat, poultry, or eggs. The danger lies in using possibly contaminated knives and cutting boards for fruits, vegetables, or bread. If the foods are not cooked, the germs are not killed. Throw away all those wooden cutting boards and get plastic ones that can be washed in the dishwasher after use. Don't forget to clean your can opener periodically.

Never defrost meat, poultry, or fish on a kitchen counter. Plan ahead so you can defrost it in the refrigerator, or defrost it in the microwave oven and cook it immediately.

When cooking, make sure the internal temperature is high enough to cook the food all the way through. Meat products and seafood should not be eaten raw and should be cooked to the proper temperature. For many meats, requesting "rare" or even "medium rare" could present a problem.

Having eggs "over easy" is another health threat today. There is a significant increase in cases of poisoning from salmonella bacteria found in eggs and products made with raw eggs. Do not use cracked eggs or recipes that call for raw eggs (ice cream, hollandaise, salad dressings). Soft- or medium-boiled eggs can be risky; cook scrambled and poached and fried eggs until they are no longer runny.

Always put directly into the refrigerator leftovers and foods that you have cooked and don't plan to use right away. Use the food within two to three days. Never partially cook food before storing.

Regularly take stock of what you have in your refrigerator and throw away anything you are unsure of. It is better to be safe than sorry. If you have any reservations, throw it away.

Commercial mayonnaise and salad dressings contain acids, such as lemon juice and salt, that somewhat retard bacterial growth. These are not the "bad guys" like homemade mayonnaise and salad dressings.

Marinades are called for in many meat and poultry recipes, but they often do not give adequate directions for their use. Marinate in a glass dish in the refrigerator, never out on the counter. It is best to throw away the excess marinade, because it will contain blood from the raw meat. If you do want to use it, cook it to a boil before serving. Remember, all fresh food must be washed thoroughly with water and scrub brush, but no soap. Canned goods containers must be inspected for dents, bulges, and leaks.

What about storage and the good old pantry? All households used to have a room that was designed specifically to store provisions and food. It's fortunate to have a walk-in pantry, but everyone has cupboards or storage shelves. We might not want to go to the store as often and we feel secure in case of emergency to have things on hand.

Few of us find ourselves running out of staples, but from time to time check your supply of dried staples, such as sugar, flour, baking soda and powder, dried milk, and spices and herbs. Also, rice, pastas, and boxed convenience foods. Do you have a variety of canned soups, meats, fish, fruits, and vegetables on hand? Your refrigerator and freezer also should be part of your pantry and contain long lasting items for an emergency.

We have only touched briefly on this important subject of food safety and storage. As you get older, your digestive and immune system is not as efficient and it is imperative that you are more cautious with food safety.

The United States Department of Agriculture has a toll-free Meat and Poultry Hotline (800-535-4555) to answer many questions on the proper handling of meat and poultry. You also can request booklets on food safety. If you need to report food-related illnesses, call the Consumer Product Safety Commission at 1-800-638-2772.

31

MODIFYING RECIPES/COOKING METHODS

Remember the "good old days" of fried chicken, fried potatoes, cookies, cakes, and pies every day, 8–10 ounce servings of meat, everything slathered in rich sauces, gravies, and butter! I am sure you can recollect spending many hours in the kitchen preparing the food I just described.

The vision of an older person resistant to change certainly is not true when it comes to shopping, cooking, and eating. The many fitness and nutrition classes I have had the privilege of teaching for the fifty-plus gang over the past 20 years certainly has disputed this perception. Even though most of us learned this type of cooking and eating via our families, I have found the older we get, perhaps the more adaptable to change we become.

Ask yourself how can I alter, vary, moderate, reduce, lessen, transform, convert, adjust, eliminate, and substitute? How can I cut down on fat, sugar, sodium, and calories? And how can I add fiber and more complex carbohydrates and make our food appealing, satisfying, and just plain good-tasting? It is a creative art that is challenging and fun. There are many current recipe books that take the guesswork out of it for you, but here are some suggestions to get you started on your own. Let's look at the food groups and decide what simple procedures we can follow to make some positive changes.

Meat group: Buy the leanest cut of meat possible. Ring the bell at the meat counter and let your butcher help you select lean beef, pork, and lamb. Understanding the labeling of percentage of fat in meat is tricky. Eighty percent lean by weight is 20 percent fat by weight. This actually calculates out to 36 percent of calories provided from fat. What you should look for is 85 percent lean or a higher percentage. Make poultry and fish a big part of your weekly menu plans. Remove all visible fat from meat before cooking. Research has shown that chicken skin is a high source of monounsaturated fats. Buying boneless skinless chicken at five times the price of regular chicken is not necessary. To cut the consumption of fat, use cooking methods such as roasting, braising, and grilling. Try to limit your portions to 3 ounces.

Dairy group: Many adjustments can be made in this group. Whenever a recipe calls for milk or cream, use powdered skim milk or evaporated skim milk. Substitute sour cream with plain drained nonfat yogurt. Select low-fat cheeses. Part-skim ricotta cheese and low-fat cottage cheese can be used in place of cream cheese. Don't give up drinking milk, just switch to skim. Try nonfat frozen yogurt. Use two egg whites instead of a whole egg.

Fruit and vegetable group: The complex carbohydrates is the group where you can increase your dietary fiber. The natural sweetness in fruits can help that sweet tooth. You can substitute applesauce for sugar in many baked goods and use sweet spices and vanilla for additional flavoring. This may help to lose some of the desire to eat the "empty calorie" sweets, such as candy, cookies, and pies. Use twice as many vegetables as the recipe calls for and cut down on the amount of meat in a recipe. Snack on crunchy vegetables instead of high-fat chips with excessive sodium. Use tomato juice and lemon for salad dressings and seasonings. Look for oil-free salad dressings.

Bread and cereal group: This is another area from which you can increase your intake of complex carbohydrates. Breads, cereals, rice, and pastas are not in themselves fattening. It is what you add to all of these super good foods that contribute too much fat, sugar, and sodium. Use low-fat and low-sugar spreads for your breads. There is a variety of natural fruit spreads to choose from. Eat your cereals with low-fat milk and fruit for sweetening. Read the cereal labels. You want less than 6–8 grams simple sugars or sucrose and no frosted cereals. Watch those sauces on your rice and pasta dishes.

What about other areas of caution? Sugar, salt, and especially fat are used for flavor and texture in foods. The additions of these substances to our foods is from habit and the acquired tastes we have formed over the years. Sugar, salt, and fat can disguise the real taste of the food. Try no crust or graham cracker crust pies.

Also watch the added sodium in condiments, such as mustard, ketchup, and soy sauces. Use salt cautiously while cooking or eating. Nuts and seeds are high in fat and should be decreased in recipes. Also decrease the amount of sugar and fat in all of your recipes.

Have supplies in your pantry and refrigerator that will make it easy to convert and change recipes. Here is a partial list: applesauce, plain yogurt, dried milk, spices and herbs, vanilla and other flavorings, tomato juice, low-fat margarine, egg substitutes, low-fat cheeses, and lemon juice.

Learn to use the nonstick cookware and nonstick spray for your pans instead of using shortening. Instead of frying, poach or steam in water or broth.

Some of the recipes can be tricky and if you are insecure and fear you might have a failure, there are plenty of cookbooks to make it easier for you. More and more newspaper and magazine food columns feature recipe modifications; there are many cooking classes available. We are never too old to make those changes that can enhance the quality of our lives. There is much talk today of "comfort food," and what could make us feel more content, satisfied, and secure than to know the changes we make are better for ourselves and our families, plus setting a good example for the younger generation.

32

COOKING FOR ONE OR TWO

The title of this Key could be planning for one or two. The secret to cooking for one or two is *organization* and *planning*. If you spend the most time planning, you then can spend much less time shopping, preparing, and cooking. A recent Good Housekeeping Institute Survey of Food Trends found that people are looking for two words in dining: "fast" and "healthy." Even though we in the over fifty set may not be as busy with home, family, and career, those two words fit the description of what we want also. In addition, we could add "economical." Perhaps you have an empty nest, are a single career person, have never had children, or have lost a spouse. There are many reasons to make cooking at this stage of life both fun and challenging. This is the time of life that men often discover cooking is fun even when it is sometimes out of necessity. It is never too late to learn.

The Keys on budgeting, menu planning, grocery lists, and shopping are very important. Don't forget to check the newspaper specials, your supply of coupons, and the amount of money you have budgeted for grocery shopping. If you qualify for food stamps, by all means use them. To find out if you qualify, get in touch with your local Department of Social Services. So you won't catch yourself impulse buying, always shop with a list and never shop when you are hungry!

Many supermarkets are now accommodating that big group of one or two in a household by offering single-serving items. Canned goods offer the largest selection from which to choose, but can be more costly than buying in a larger quantity. If your supermarket has a deli, salad bar, and bakery, take advantage of buying just the amount you need. Ask the produce and meat employees to repackage an item that is too large for your use.

Frozen vegetables in large bags are economical and you can use small amounts at a time. Sometimes you can share large portions of food with a neighbor or friend. As a single or a couple you will not be using food as expeditiously now, so be sure to check expiration and freshness dates.

The kitchen of today with all of its modern conveniences is very adaptable to cooking in small portions. The freezer is wonderful for storing a variety of food. You must be practical too. Large freezers use a lot of electricity, thus your public service bill will be higher. Sometimes I get so much bread from the day-old bread store, my husband calls our freezer a very expensive bread box! It is best to go shopping more frequently for your produce for it to retain its freshness. When staples have been opened, it is best to store them in the refrigerator to maintain the freshest flavor.

There are many very good recipe books available on cooking for one or two. Many newspapers and magazines feature columns with recipes for one or two. If mathematics is not a problem, you can take your standard recipe and decrease all of the ingredients, although doing so sometimes does not yield the desired results. It is fun to devise your own recipes.

The microwave and toaster ovens are wonderful for small portions. Stir frying is a fast and nutritious method of cooking using a Chinese wok or skillet. It is a good way to use leftovers and you can cook only the portion you can eat.

Casseroles, stews, and soups are conducive to cooking in a larger quantity and freezing what you do not need for a later date. Be sure to wrap the food adequately and always mark your frozen foods with the date so you do not keep them too long. Also, make muffins, biscuits, pancakes, and waffles in larger portions and then freeze them in individual servings.

You can fix a big Sunday dinner, such as turkey, roasts, and all of the trimmings, and make your own frozen dinners with the leftovers. I freeze food in small portions on a cookie sheet, cover them with freezer wrap, and then bag for handiness. Make sure you do not leave anything in your freezer too long on the tray or in the bag, because freezer burn can dry out and destroy the freshness and the nutrients.

Ethnic foods lend themselves to smaller portions. Look at the possibilities with Mexican, Chinese, Italian, other Mediterranean foods (French, Spanish, Turkish, and Greek), and foods from different regions of the United States. An interesting new world of cooking for one or two can open up to you. Take advantage of ethnic cooking classes in your area.

Yes, I admit, we can all get bored, run out of ideas, and make excuses for not cooking at home. I hope some of these thoughts will spark your imagination and you will explore new ideas in your kitchen.

33

APPETITE/EATING ALONE/
EATING ALTERNATIVES

Over a lifetime, there are many changes in our appetite and desire to eat. There is a joy and delight in seeing a baby take its first solid food. Can you recall teenage boys' stomachs being a bottomless pit? I am sure all of you can recall many examples of young and old, healthy and sick having variations in appetite. Review your own eating patterns over the years, and assess where you are right now with them. Some people reading this book will be looking for a secret to decreasing their appetite and losing weight, and others will be at the stage in life where their appetite is waning and they need to stabilize or gain weight.

A five-year project by the Nutrition Screening Initiative is appraising the nation's eating habits. The survey of 802 Americans age sixty-five and older found that one in five skips at least one meal a day. This is a great risk for poor nutrition. Some of the reasons given were that they lived alone, did not want to cook for themselves, had a loss of appetite, had lost their sense of taste because of medications taken, and could not afford to purchase adequate food. Do you, or does anyone you know, fall into any of these categories?

Food usually is associated with warm, positive thoughts and memories. It is associated with happy times and places. As we age, food and eating can lose a prominent position in our lives.

One of the biggest complaints from the people in my nutrition classes is that they do not like to eat alone. Following are some ideas for improving your appetite and making dining alone more pleasurable.

If you are losing weight unintentionally, be sure to see your doctor to determine what the problem might be. There are many medical reasons that could be causing the difficulty, including undetected illnesses and diseases, drug and medication interactions, dry mouth, and depression. To gain weight, try larger portions and higher calorie and nutritionally dense foods. Try snacking during the day and drinking liquid nutritional supplements. (Don't worry, we will address weighing too much in Key 36!)

Serve food that you really like and is good for you. Do not skip meals; plan for every single meal ahead of time. Try eating several small mini-meals instead of the standard three meals a day. Choose a different place to eat such as by a window or on the patio with music or a good book. Have an attractive table setting, placemat or tablecloth, cloth napkin, flowers, candles, nice dishes, and silverware. Brush your teeth before meals. Remember, you are not being extravagant because there is just you! You are the most important person you know.

Some other eating alternatives are to start a pot-luck group or gourmet club. Invite friends to join you. Check to see if you are qualified for Meals-on-Wheels. Contact your local Volunteers of America for congregate dining centers and delivery of meals to your home. Check into meals at your local senior citizen center. Prepare new foods and have a tasting party. Try new recipes from different countries once a week.

Many people who have lost a spouse tell me the most difficult time of the day is mealtime. No more communication and sharing. This would be a time to develop some of the preceding ideas and expand on others that you may have.

Safety first is important when you live alone. Pay close attention to all precautions when preparing and cooking (see Key 29). Because there is no one to assist you if you have breathing or choking difficulties, take care when eating. Aspiration occurs when material passes through the larynx and enters the lungs. Cut your food in small sizes, chew thoroughly and slowly. Make sure you have completely swallowed your food before taking another bite or talking. If possible, be near a telephone when you are eating in case trouble arises.

Many books have been written on cooking and eating with disabilities, such as results of a stroke, arthritis, loss of sight and hearing, confinement to a wheelchair, and so on. If you have a disability, be sure to get an evaluation from your doctor. He then can recommend that you get an assessment from an occupational therapist on making life easier in your kitchen. There are so many techniques, including unique utensils and equipment, to make food preparation, service, and cleanup effortless. An occupational therapist is a wonderful friend who certainly can improve the quality of your life and keep you safe and independent.

Growth is a part of life. Perhaps this Key will assist you in seeking alternatives to some negatives in your living situation, and turning them into positives. This way you can lead a fuller and richer life with each passing year.

34

DINING OUT

At this stage of life we do not want to spend the majority of our time in the kitchen, so let's go out on the town! We should think of eating as a dining experience, whether it is at home or in a restaurant. What a selection of establishments we have to choose from today. There are mom and pop cafés, fancy expensive restaurants where dining really is an art, fast foods, ethnic types, cafeterias, chain restaurants, steak houses, seafood restaurants, pizza parlors, convenience stores, and so on. Whatever your mood, you usually can make a good choice. Many times with the senior set, dining out is a social event; the experience itself is as important as the food we eat.

Can you eat out and still maintain a healthy diet? That depends on how often you eat out, where you eat, what you eat, and how much you order. Eating out is a very individual matter and these are just general guidelines to help you make wise choices. Contact your local American Heart Association for a listing of "healthy heart" restaurants in your vicinity.

When eating out, you should follow the same dietary guidelines you do when you are eating at home. Take into consideration variety, moderation, and balance. Do not just load up when you go out to eat.

Take time to study the menu before you order. The secret is planning before you order. Do not be afraid to ask your waiter how things are prepared, if you can make special requests, and if smaller portions are available. If the portions are too large, be sure to request a "doggie" bag. In fact, get the doggie bag before you start eating. These general guidelines can hold true for eating breakfast, lunch, or dinner out. It is becoming popular with older adults to have their main meal at noon. A very healthy choice.

For an appetizer, choose vegetables or fruit, or perhaps a vegetable or fruit juice cocktail. When choosing soups, stay away from the cream soups, for they are high in fat. Choose a broth based soup, but be aware of the sodium content. Ask for a cup of soup instead of a bowl. Try to choose a fresh fruit salad without any added ingredients. Or perhaps a tossed salad, but ask for the salad dressing on the side or request a low-fat salad dressing. Be selective; use your willpower if they bring a tempting basket of bread to the table. Again, it is what you put on the bread—such as butter and high-sugared jams and jellies—that is detrimental. Try bread or rolls with nothing on them. Sometimes a hearty soup and a salad will suffice.

Now for the main course. Select a small cut of meat, poultry, or fish, preferably no more than 3 ounces. Try to have it broiled, grilled, baked, steamed, or poached. If you do have something fried or breaded, remove the skin and the breading.

The starchy food that accompanies the entrée usually is good for you, even baked potato, rice, and pasta. Again, it is what you put on it that is nonnutritious. If a dinner comes with french fries, you often can substitute a salad or more vegetables. You can request that your vegetables be prepared without butter, salt, or sauces.

The dessert menus always are tempting. Naturally, the best choice of dessert is fresh fruit, sherbet, sorbet, or fruit ice. If you must have something sweet, share one dessert with the whole table, or be satisfied with an after dinner mint. The beverage of choice to begin and end the meal should be water.

What about eating out in ethnic type restaurants? Mexican, French, Chinese, and Italian foods can be healthy, but also very high in fat and sodium. Try to avoid anything fried or deep-fried, with added condiments and sauces. Many times you feel more in control by fixing ethnic foods in your own kitchen.

Does fast food mean fat food? Not necessarily. Being selective in choosing the fast-food restaurant is important. The reputation of this type of restaurant being junk food for the younger set no longer is valid. Many older adults find this type

110

of restaurant to be convenient, economical, dependable, and have good service. Fast-food restaurants can provide essential nutrients and many of them are adding salad bars and low-fat products and cooking. So, we have healthier choices in all food groups. Some of them are giving nutritional information regarding calories, fat, and sodium. These foods, though, can be lacking in fiber and some of the vitamins. Just like any type of dining, you must use discretion. This is an area where you need to do some investigating and research.

What a great time of life to travel, whether by car, train, plane, or ship. Many of us used to believe that if you did not gain some weight on a trip, you did not have a good time! What a difference in thinking these days. There is no need to forsake good eating while on a trip. When my husband and I travel by car, we carry a cooler and picnic basket for our breakfasts and lunches. We do not overindulge for dinner, and eat early so we can take a walk afterwards. Train dining can be as elegant as it used to be, but I am sure the railroads also have made advances toward healthier preparation and cooking methods.

The airlines are very willing to honor special food requests. If at all possible, inform them when you make your reservations or at least 48 hours in advance of your departure. They have available diabetic, low-cholesterol, low-fat, vegetarian, and kosher meals. Because exercise is at a minimum on an airplane, the meal portions have been downsized. There are also major changes in food service on cruise ships, which used to be associated with "all you can eat," almost on a 24-hour basis, and taken advantage of because it already was paid for. Now in our "old" age, perhaps we have acquired some common sense and know that discretion is the better part of valor. The cruise lines have made healthy menus and exercise readily available.

All of us want to be in control of our diets whether at home or dining out. The restaurateurs are listening to our concerns and helping to make dining out healthy and enjoyable for all.

35

CELEBRATIONS

Celebrations! Many times celebrations and traditions go hand in hand. What is the first thing we think about? *Food*, of course! What are we going to serve, what are we going to have to eat? Pause and reflect on the many celebrations you have participated in over your lifetime. Births, birthdays, weddings, anniversaries, Mother's Day, Father's Day, Valentine's Day, St. Patrick's Day, Fourth of July, Thanksgiving, Christmas, Hanukkah, retirements, promotions, new homes, sporting events, bon voyage, graduations, welcome home. Even a quiet evening alone can be a celebration. Aren't memories wonderful at this stage of life? What would a party be without food? Pretty dull and boring, right?

Most of the following pointers can be adjusted to any type of celebration and any type of meal. They are adaptable whether you are cooking and entertaining at home or invited out. These suggestions can be used for breakfast, morning coffees, brunch, lunches, afternoon tea, cocktails, and dinner parties. The primary consideration is balance and moderation. Plan ahead and do not neglect the food groups, concentrate on the nutrient dense foods, and eat less of the empty calorie foods.

If you are going out, eat or drink something before you leave home. A glass of water or low-fat milk and a piece of whole wheat bread or cereal will curb your appetite. When you get to a party, survey the food table and preplan what you are going to eat, concentrating on fresh fruits and vegetables and leaving the rich dips alone. If possible, socialize for a while instead of heading for the buffet. Be the last in line instead of the first. Fix your own drink, on the light side if possible. Nonalcoholic beverages, such as fruit juices or water, are better than alcohol.

If you do have an alcoholic drink, make it last a long time and alternate with nonalcoholic drinks.

It is important to keep reminding ourselves that one of the big culprits in all eating is fat intake. Our diet should contain no more than 30 percent of daily calories in fat. Some experts lower that to 20 percent. So, it behooves you when celebrating to watch those fat calories. Sodium and sugar also can cause concern. Another way to cut back is to serve fewer courses and smaller portions. There are many good entertaining cookbooks on the market or you can alter your favorite recipes. Try to find recipes that can be made ahead of time and frozen. You want to enjoy your own parties, too.

Many of us never have lost "the child within us," including me. When it comes to any holiday, I am ready to go all out to make it special. The past few years I have tried to put more effort into decorating the house rather than decorating the food with extras that we do not need. It is reported that during a special holiday, you can consume 5,000 to 7,000 calories and gain five to seven pounds. Following are some recommendations to help you make all of your holidays happy, healthy, and hardy.

Purchase a plain turkey; it contains less fat and is cheaper. Stay away from the self-basting varieties. When serving the turkey, remember that white meat has fewer calories and less fat than the dark meat. (However, the difference is insignificant, so enjoy whichever you prefer.) Always remove the skin. You can get the same flavor in poultry dressing by omitting the butter and eggs and baste with broth. Add more celery and onions to the bread crumbs. Sauté the celery and onions in water or broth instead of butter or margarine. If you cook the dressing separately, it will not absorb the fat from the turkey and there is less risk for food poisoning. After roasting the turkey, drain off the drippings, let the fat rise, refrigerate, and skim it off. Just use the juices for the gravy. Use powdered nonfat milk in the mashed potatoes and omit the salt and butter. The gravy is usually flavorful enough. Use herbs, spices, and lemon on your vegetables instead of rich sauces or canned soups. In salads, use 1 percent cottage cheese rather than cream cheese. Make your own cranberry sauce. The canned variety is loaded with sugar. Try crustless pumpkin pie and use powdered milk and just one egg yolk.

I am sure all of you could contribute your own special family recipes you have modified to the "new" way of thinking. I hope these tips will spur you on to make all of your celebrations joyous, nutritious, and delicious.

36

WEIGHT CONTROL AND MAINTENANCE

Perhaps you can relate to this Key better than the Key on loss of appetite and weight. Weight loss, weight control, and weight maintenance are ongoing concerns and vary from individual to individual. Each person's weight depends on age, sex, state of health, and activity level. Other contributing factors are heredity, family history and background, and environment. Like other topics in this book, much research and studies constantly are being done on this subject.

Are there differences in nutritional requirements as we get older? Yes, there are differences between young, middle age, older adults, and the elderly regarding nutrition and weight control. At this time, the amount of nutrients to stay healthy is about the same for everyone over fifty. New studies are on the horizon showing that we need to divide the groups into smaller segments according to age.

We do know that as we get older, our bodies carry more fat deposits and the lean muscle mass decreases. The more body fat we have, the less efficient at burning calories the body becomes. Lean muscle mass burns more calories. That is why it is imperative to make every calorie count and eat nutrient-dense foods and leave the empty calories alone. Activity and exercise burn calories; many times older adults reduce their activity level. This is due partly to health problems and partly to the "rocking chair" and "couch potato" syndrome.

Obesity is considered to occur when the scale registers 20 to 30 percent above a person's ideal weight resulting in an accumulation of excessive body fat. *Overweight* is a body weight of 10 percent above ideal weight. Ideal weight is different for everyone. The body is composed of water, fat, muscle, and bones. Sixty percent of a person's weight is water, the rest is fat and muscle, and a very small percentage of weight is bone.

We do need a certain amount of body fat. It gives us energy, prevents excessive heat loss in cold weather, maintains healthy skin and hair, and protects the body's organs from injury.

However, the risks of too much body fat outweigh the benefits. Some of the possible risks are heart disease, high blood pressure, diabetes, high cholesterol levels, circulatory problems, and higher risk of some forms of cancer. Add to that gallbladder problems, arthritis, more susceptibility to infections, lack of energy, tiring easily, difficulty breathing, inability to participate in exercises, difficulties with surgery, poor mobility, back problems, liver ailments, and joint problems leading to arthritis. It also results in low self-esteem, and lack of motivation, which can affect your personality and relationships. Have I missed anything? You probably can add to this list by personal retrospection.

If you read the information in Keys 1 through 35 and followed it, we would not need a chapter on weight control. But no one is perfect! Most of the students in my nutrition classes over the past 20 years signed up initially to lose weight. The key to weight loss, control, and maintenance is to *decrease* the amount of food you eat and *increase* your physical activity. Add to that the intention to lose weight, sound nutrition education, and self-discipline. Sounds simple, yet no one has found the ultimate secret of success.

The diet business is a billion dollar industry. No one plan works for everyone. There are numerous books, classes, and methods from which to choose. When selecting a diet plan, it should be nutritionally safe and include varied menus selected from the four food groups. It should not drastically cut calorie consumption, but should include an exercise program. Stay away from liquid diets. Fad diets do not work. Many times a support group is valuable. You always should check with your doctor before starting any weight loss program. A safe weight loss is one pound a week. To achieve that goal, cut 500 calories a day from your food intake or burn 500 calories by exercising or by a combination. To lose one pound of fat a week, it is necessary to reduce intake by 3,500 calories a week.

I am sure you know if you need to lose weight. Not just by the scale and tape measure, or how your clothes fit, and if you have any minor or major health problems. The best way to evaluate your present lifestyle is to keep a daily diary. Ideal weight is weight you feel best at, and is particularly true with older people. Get a calorie counting book and write down what you eat, the amount and the calories. Also keep track of the quantity of water you drink and the type and total time you exercise. Keeping a diary is a very important step toward weight loss and should be done on a regular basis throughout your life to maintain your proper weight. Remember, you do not go on or off a diet but are on a diet continuously through life. Sometimes it is a high quality diet, other times it is unsatisfactory. The on-again, off-again weight loss approach is a greater danger than being a few pounds above what you perceive as normal.

The word *diet* itself is self defeating. The word implies you are going to eat a certain way for a period of time, lose a few pounds, and then go back to how you usually eat and gain it back. To lose weight and keep it off, you have to change habits and lifestyle.

The benefits of maintaining a desirable weight are numerous. Review the risks, then write down all of the rewards you can think of that would help you or someone you know benefit from a weight control program.

Proper weight control is a lifetime commitment, but well worth the time and effort. It can improve the quantity of your years and the quality of your life. Good luck!

37

BEHAVIOR MODIFICATION

Every one of us can use many different excuses for not being at the proper weight. It is heredity, old age, metabolism, and so on. The biggest obstacle in the control of our weight is detrimental behavior that has become a habit. This is where behavior modification comes into play. It is the ability to change some form of our behavior: replacing a "bad" habit with a "good" habit; reinforcing positive behavior and eliminating negative behavior; retraining your present conduct. You must alter your lifestyle, change your attitudes, and set realistic goals. We can use behavior modification with all types of addictions and bad habits.

Time for another list. Get out your paper and pencil and record the behavior modification techniques you can use to improve your eating and to help you with weight control. Following are some random ideas and thoughts to get you started on your own inventory.

Set realistic goals. Evaluate your present nutrition status. Have planned menus and scheduled mealtimes. Do not skip breakfast. Plan your snack ahead of time. Are you eating for emotional reasons? Are you really hungry? Do not buy tempting food or have it in the house. Replace junk food with low-calorie snacks. Keep a food diary. Learn to count calories. Weigh and measure your portions. Cut down on portion size. Use a small plate. Do not put serving dishes on the table so you will be tempted to have seconds. Play soft, slow, soothing music while you are eating. Do not taste while cooking and baking. Always sit down to eat. Put your fork down between bites. Dine in a specified place and do not deviate. Drink plenty of water and other low-calorie liquids. This will give you a sense of fullness. *Exercise!*

Also, eat slowly. Avoid nibbling while watching TV. Do something with your hands. Get at least 30 minutes of exercise daily. Do not forsake getting plenty of calcium-rich foods. Plan activities if you are bored, instead of eating to relieve boredom. Learn to cook the low-fat and no-fat way. Eat slowly. Chew thoroughly. When eating out, order an appetizer and salad instead of the main course. Put half your meal in a "doggie" bag before you start eating. Ask for salad dressing on the side. Remove the saltshakers from your table at home. Learn when your appetite is satisfied and stop eating. Try several small meals. Eat your big meal at noon. *Exercise!*

Learn deep breathing techniques, some good stretches, and relaxing techniques. In fact, exercise along with me on my video, "More Alive Fitness For Mature Adults." Be more active. Unless preparing a meal, stay out of the kitchen. This will help you avoid food temptations. Try some new low-calorie cookbooks. Take a fitness class. Go dancing. Have short-term goals. Don't cook more than you need for a particular meal. If you do overindulge don't feel guilty, just cut back the next day. Eat your favorite food in small amounts. Use caffeine and alcohol in moderation. Use salt sparingly. Don't shop when you are hungry. *Exercise!*

You get the idea. You must retrain your eating habits. Implement these behavior modification practices slowly, not all at once. Keep repeating to yourself, "I am now in control."

38

DIGESTIVE DISEASES/
DISORDERS/DEFICIENCIES

It sometimes is difficult to distinguish between a digestive disease, disorder, and deficiency. A *disease* is a condition of the living animal that impairs the performance of a vital function. A *disorder* is an abnormal physical or mental condition. A *deficiency* is a shortage of substances necessary to health. As you can see, they are all interrelated. Let's examine various conditions that might be related to nutrition, digestion, and age.

Digestion is a complex process that occurs after chewing food. The food passes into the stomach, then enters the small intestine. The digested food passes into the lower part of the small intestine where nutrients are transported into the blood. The remainder of the food material is pushed into the colon, part of the large intestine, where water is removed before the resulting waste is eliminated.

As you age, your body sometimes begins to work less efficiently and you may have digestive problems. The action of the muscles of the digestive track may be slower. There may be a decreased secretion of stomach acid resulting in a poor absorption of the vital nutrients. Changes in lifestyle, such as increased use of medicines and changes in eating habits, can cause some concerns. If you are worried that you might have a digestive disease, disorder, or deficiency, make sure you see a health care professional for proper diagnosis and treatment. Trying to diagnose or treat yourself may upset the balance of the various body systems.

Some of the warning signs that might indicate that you may have a digestive difficulty and need to see your doctor are: pain in any part of your digestive system, such as mouth, throat, stomach, small or large intestine; change in bowel habits and consistency of stools; vomiting blood or finding blood in the stools; unexplained weight loss or gain; difficulty swallowing food; and fevers and chills.

The causes of many digestive difficulties are unknown. Besides constipation and diarrhea, what other conditions might cause concern? **Diverticulosis**—Small sacs form on the wall of the large intestine. **Gallbladder**—Stones can form in the gallbladder. **Gas**—May be caused by eating high fiber foods or a lactose intolerance, and affects everyone differently. **Heartburn**—A pain behind the breastbone occurring after meals caused by certain foods. May be symptomatic of a hiatal hernia. **Hemorrhoids**—Caused by pressure in the rectal veins commonly due to constipation or obesity. **Hiatal hernia**—Part of the stomach slides up through the diaphragm and can cause the stomach acid to back up. **Indigestion**—A number of symptoms such as nausea, vomiting, bloating, and abdominal pain. This can be related to other digestive disorders. **Lactose intolerance**—Inability to digest milk and milk products. **Ulcerative colitis**—Parts of the large intestine become inflamed. This is a partial list of some of the digestive concerns as you age.

Nutrition has a profound influence on other processes of your body, such as circulatory, respiratory, nervous, and immune systems. Thus it is vitally imperative to place strong emphasis on good nutrition as you get older.

A healthful diet also helps to control, and under some circumstances, eliminate stress-related disorders such as ulcers, hypertension, migraine headaches, and heart irregularities. Food from each of the major food groups should be consumed to diminish having to be concerned with stress-related illnesses. Many times stress leads us to eat empty, junk type foods instead of the nutritious dense kind.

Legitimate vitamin and mineral deficiencies are rare, but borderline malnutrition can be common. There are numerous physiological, sociological, and psychological factors that affect the nutrition status of the older person. Some of these undernutrition and overnutrition symptoms can be lethargy, irritability, weight loss or gain, weakness, insomnia, or excessive desire for sleep.

The bottom line is a well-balanced diet, using common sense and moderation. Prevention can be the answer to many of these anxieties. Be sure to discuss any digestive concerns with your doctor. Evaluation should include diet history, medical and drug history, and a complete physical examination.

Many of these areas reflect back to childhood and the traits and characteristics with which you were raised. Think back to your ancestry, family life, work pattern, and social life. You will learn a tremendous amount about your present habits and difficulties related to eating. Understanding these factors can contribute to making a positive change in possible long-established detrimental habits.

39

HEART DISEASE

The next five Keys will be devoted to an overview of five conditions that are affected greatly by diet and age. They are heart disease, cancer, diabetes, hypertension, and stroke. As the older population grows in numbers, the incidence of these conditions will expand. No one is free from the possibility of contracting any of these diseases.

Heart disease is still the number one killer of Americans. The most common form of heart disease is atherosclerotic blockage of the coronary arteries. *Atherosclerosis* is a process in which the lining of the arteries becomes coated with fat deposits. For prevention and treatment of cardiovascular diseases, it is important to know as much about them as possible. Consult with your doctor and the American Heart Association for excellent educational material.

The risk factors are familiar to all of us. They include: elevated cholesterol levels, high blood pressure, a sedentary lifestyle, a diet high in fat and low in fiber, obesity, high intake of fat and cigarette smoking, lack of exercise, high level of stress, and diabetes. How many of these risk factors do you have?

Add to these risks such things as heredity. What is the family history of heart disease? Environment and your overall lifestyle are other factors that affect diseases.

Research has proved that we can reverse and halt heart disease. Some of the changes are to reduce your total cholesterol, keep your blood pressure within a normal range, keep your blood sugar levels within a normal range, do heart-strengthening exercises, keep your weight within a normal range, do not smoke, avoid too much alcohol, and control excessive stress in your life.

Many of the risk factors can be completely eradicated with a change in your diet. If you would follow most of the prior Keys in this book, you would be conforming to a healthy heart diet. There is no secret formula, it is very simple. Follow the four food groups, eat a variety of foods and eat in moderation. Review all of the Keys, especially the ones on fat and cholesterol. We need to keep our daily fat intake below 30 percent, limit saturated fat intake to less than 10 percent, and strive for balance in diet.

Much research is now being done on the benefits of omega-3's fatty acids found in cold-water fish. It seems apparent that these are found in seafood, canola oil, and some other sources. Omega-3's seem to lower triglycerides. Because these studies are as yet inconclusive, nutritionists do not recommend taking fish oil supplements. However, it seems wise to include more seafood in our diet.

A few years ago, this Key could have been titled "for men only to read." There was a myth that women were virtually immune from heart disease. Now it is known that women are just as susceptible to it as men. Females do not have as great a risk as males until a later age. But, with life expectancy rising annually and women living longer than men, they need to take all of the same precautions.

By reading *Keys to Fitness Over Fifty*, you will realize the importance of exercise in preventing many negative signs of aging. Your exercise goal for a healthy heart should be to gradually work up to 20 to 30 minutes of aerobic exercise at least three times a week. Another important contribution to a healthy heart is to learn how to relax and control your stress.

Your objective should be to take charge of your life and do as much as you can to prevent and reverse heart disease by making changes in your lifestyle. Sign up for a heart-healthy cooking class. Get more information from your local American Heart Association. It is never too late to learn and grow. Start today.

40

CANCER

Every person seems somehow to be touched by cancer—you personally, a family member, a dear friend, a neighbor, or an acquaintance. *Cancer* is a disease in which cells grow abnormally. The cells can continue to grow and eventually invade healthy tissue. Many cancers occur more often in people age fifty or older than in other age groups. The risk of cancer increases in older persons because many forms of cancer have long latent periods, and aging appears to make a person more susceptible to carcinogens. It is important that we learn as much about the disease as we can. It is a dreaded and feared malady that crosses all age, sex, and race boundaries.

Prevention, detection, and treatment of cancer are all of prime importance. When cancers are detected early, successful treatment and survival definitely are enhanced. The following are some of the most common cancers and symptoms in people over age fifty:

Breast: Change in breast shape, lump in the breast, a discharge from the nipple.

Colon and rectum: Changes in bowel habits; bleeding from the rectum; bright red or black blood in the stool.

Lung: Shortness of breath, persistent cough, coughing up blood.

Prostate: Men have difficulty or pain while urinating; the need to urinate often, especially at night.

Skin: Change in color, size, and shape of a mole or wart; sudden appearance of a mole; a sore that does not heal.

Because pain often is not a primary symptom, routine health checkups are a major consideration. Even if you do not have symptoms, there are specific tests recommended. If you have a history of cancer in your family, other medical conditions, or need improvement in your lifestyle, it will behoove you to have the following tests:

Breast examination and mammography: An X ray of the breasts is recommended annually for women over age fifty. It can detect tumors even before they can be felt.

Guaiac test: A test to check for blood in the stool that can be helpful in detecting colon or rectal cancer.

Pelvic examination and Pap smear: A check of the female reproductive organs is recommended once or twice a year, depending on age, heredity factors, menopause history, estrogen therapy, and so on.

Rectal exams: This can detect prostate tumors in men and rectal tumors in women and men.

Sigmoidoscopy: An examination of the rectum and part of the colon.

Some of the risk factors and prevention guidelines for cancer are similar to the ones for heart disease. Do not smoke, maintain desirable weight, exercise daily, know your family history of diseases, get regular physical checkups, avoid unnecessary X rays, make your home and place of work as healthy and safe as possible. Some of these factors are not controllable and can't be changed. It is important, though, to control the ones that you can. Most important is *diet*.

Nutrition and Your Health: Dietary Guidelines for Americans was written by the U.S. Department of Agriculture and U.S. Department of Health and Human Services and National Cancer Institute. This publication gives some simple guidelines for a healthy cancer prevention diet:

• Eat a variety of foods. No one food provides all the nutrients that a person needs. It is important to eat a wide variety each day from the four food groups.
• Maintain desirable weight. Obesity is a risk factor for many diseases, including heart disease, high blood pressure, diabetes, and some cancers.

- Avoid too much fat, saturated fat, and cholesterol. A diet low in total fat may reduce the risk for cancers of the breast, prostate, colon, and rectum.
- Eat foods with adequate starch and fiber. Health experts recommend that we increase the amount of starch and fiber in our diets by eating more fruits, vegetables, potatoes, whole grain bread and cereals, and dry peas and beans. A high fiber diet may reduce the risk of colon and rectal cancer.
- Eat diets rich in foods containing vitamin A, vitamin C, and a precursor of vitamin A called beta carotene.
- Include cruciferous vegetables. They not only are good sources of fiber and some vitamins and minerals, but also are believed to reduce cancer risk. These are vegetables from the cabbage family, including broccoli, brussels sprouts, cabbage, and cauliflower. And do not forget all of the greens!
- If you drink alcoholic beverages, do so in moderation. Heavy drinking is associated with cancers of the mouth, throat, esophagus, and liver.

Extreme fear of cancer can cause paranoia and hypochondria, and should be controlled. Also, do not allow yourself to feel guilty if you or someone you know is diagnosed with cancer. Many people live up to the best possible lifestyle, and yet still are affected with some form of cancer.

Education is important with such a frightening disease. Obtain more detailed information on food choices, early detection, and any answers to your questions by calling the Cancer Information Service at 1-800-4-CANCER. You will be connected automatically to the Cancer Information Service serving your area.

41

DIABETES

Here we go again, same story, different verse. Much of what has been said about diet, heart disease, and cancer can be repeated when diabetes is discussed.

What exactly is diabetes? *Diabetes* (high blood sugar) occurs when the pancreas does not secrete sufficient insulin. The food eaten is broken down into a sugar called glucose. *Glucose* is the body's major source of energy. It needs the assistance of insulin to enter your bloodstream and get into the cells. When insulin production is insufficient, the glucose then builds up in the bloodstream.

It is not easily understood who is susceptible to diabetes, but heredity, weight, and age seem to be contributing influences. The likelihood of getting diabetes is greater if someone in your family has it and if your are overweight. It is more prevalent with age, because the ability of the pancreas to make insulin is reduced and can become completely nonfunctional. As people get older, many functions of the body are not as efficient and can contribute to more diseases. One of the problems of diabetics and age are the compounded problems due to poor circulation. The risk of heart disease, kidney disease, nerve damage, atherosclerosis, infections, healing, gangrene, and blindness is higher.

There are two forms of diabetes mellitus: insulin-dependent (Type I) and noninsulin-dependent (Type II). Type II or "Adult onset diabetes" usually occurs in adulthood and may be controlled by a change in lifestyle and diet. This type can frequently develop from increased weight. Body cells develop an insensitivity to insulin. It is important to get proper exercise and to keep your weight at a normal level. As with all illnesses and diseases, some form of stress control is important.

What about diet? Diet plays a significant role in diabetes. Food raises your blood sugar level, so it is important to watch how much you eat and the regularity with which you eat. It is important to be under a doctor's care at all times and, if possible, obtain the help of a registered dietitian (R.D.). R.D.s can help the person with diabetes create an individualized menu and eating plan. The goal of the plan is to control your blood glucose and blood fat levels. A monitored exercise program also is advisable.

It is vitally important to choose a balance and variety from the basic four food groups and to eat in moderation and on a schedule. Never skip meals when you have diabetes. Because people with diabetes have a greater risk of developing heart disease and/or hardening of the arteries, it is particularly critical to be on a low-fat, low-cholesterol diet. People with diabetes should eat less of the simple carbohydrates such as cookies, candy, and refined sugars. Alcohol is also a problem area with people with diabetes. They may find a diet of complex carbohydrates contained in fruits, vegetables, breads, and cereals to be of benefit. Moderation of these foods is also an important factor. A diet high in complex carbohydrates is also high is fiber. Fiber can slow down the absorption of carbohydrates and keep the blood sugar at a lower level after a meal.

A simple and effective approach to proper nutrition for diabetes is the exchange plan. The food exchange method allows a person to measure the food instead of weighing it. Also, any food may be substituted for another within the same food exchange list. This is also an approach taken in many weight loss programs. Generally, the exchange categories are meat and substitutes, milk, fat, starch/bread, vegetable/fruit, and certain free foods. It is advantageous to attend a class in your locality that is taught especially for people with diabetes. The information gained can be vital to dealing constructively with the disease.

Of course, you can choose the correct foods, but if you do not prepare them correctly all health benefits can be lost. Continue cooking the low-fat way.

As we get older, we must have our health care professionals check for signs of diabetes. With careful planning and some effort, we can prevent or keep diabetes under control. It takes diet, exercise, and perhaps some prescribed medication.

To learn more about diabetes, contact your local Diabetes Association. The American Diabetes Association publishes excellent information on diabetes, as well as nutritional guides and cookbooks. For information, write the American Diabetes Association, Diabetes Information Service Center, 1660 Duke Street, Alexandria, Virginia 22314, or phone 1-800-ADA-DISC.

42

HYPERTENSION

Another condition that is interrelated with many other aspects of diet and aging is *hypertension*—high or elevated blood pressure. *Blood pressure* is the force of blood against the walls of the arteries. This force is created by the heart as it pumps blood to all parts of the body.

It is unclear just exactly why people have elevated blood pressure, but high blood pressure adds to the workload of the heart and arteries. The heart and arteries cannot function as well because of the greater pressure of the blood moving through the arteries.

As with many other health problems, some individuals are predisposed to hypertension. It is more prevalent when there is a history of it in your family. Race is also a factor; more blacks are likely to have hypertension than whites. It is also more common in the older age groups. Because of high blood pressure, risk factors for other problems intensify. If you have hypertension you have a greater danger of having other complications, such as stroke, kidney failure, and heart trouble.

There is no cure for hypertension, but it can be diagnosed, treated, and controlled. Usually there are no symptoms, although some people complain about being dizzy or tired or experiencing headaches. These problems also could be masking other serious illnesses. The only way you can tell if your blood pressure falls within the normal range is to have it checked regularly by your doctor. To get the most reliable reading, it should be checked repeatedly. If you have been diagnosed with high blood pressure, the treatment and control can be very simple. Many of the self-help procedures will do wonders. The first thing you should do is check your lifestyle. Do you smoke, are you overweight, do you get enough exercise, do you have control of your stress, and are you eating a balanced diet?

Oftentimes if you lose weight and exercise, that can be enough to lower it without medication. However, if these measures are not effective in lowering the readings, your physician probably will resort to medication. Most medicines prescribed are mild and have few side effects.

Many, but not all, hypertensive individuals benefit from a low-fat, low-salt diet. With cardiovascular disease more prevalent in people with hypertension, it makes sense to adhere to a low-fat diet.

The controversy over salt (40 percent sodium, 60 percent chloride) in the diet is ongoing. It is not known exactly why, in some people, there is a correlation between high intake of sodium and an elevated blood pressure. Too much sodium causes the body to retain water. The volume of blood in circulation increases and in turn increases the pressure in the arteries.

Today it usually is recommended to follow a moderate restriction of salt, instead of strict salt-free eating. This is something that should be discussed with your doctor and dietitian. There is too much salt in many of the foods we consume now, so label reading is important.

Most nutritionists also recommend that you increase your intake of potassium-rich foods. There also seems to be a relationship between calcium intake and blood pressure. Individuals whose intake of calcium has been low seem to be at an increased risk of developing hypertension. So, following the recommended allowances for calcium for osteoporosis possibly could be helpful in lowering blood pressure.

For additional information concerning hypertension and its control, see Keys 2, 5, 12, 24, and 36.

43

STROKE

The occurrence of heart disease, diabetes, and hypertension (high blood pressure) intensifies as we grow older, consequently the percentage of strokes is also much higher. *Apoplexy* or stroke is a condition caused by a disturbance in blood circulation in the brain, causing unconsciousness and/or paralysis. The reason we closely align strokes with aging is that about two thirds of strokes occur in persons over age sixty-five.

There are three main types of strokes: *hemorrhagic stroke*, where the blood vessel in or around the brain breaks, spilling blood into the brain; *embolic stroke*, which can start in the heart where a piece of clot can break loose and then be carried by the bloodstream to the brain. The most common stroke and one usually age related is *thrombotic stroke*, which is caused by formation of a blood clot within a blood vessel.

The process of plaque buildup (atherosclerosis) or hardening of the arteries is a slow, progressive disease that can begin very early in life. This coronary artery disease is the cause of serious heart problems. If atherosclerosis develops in an artery that leads to the brain, the result may be a stroke.

High blood pressure can cause blood vessels to become scarred, hardened, and narrow. The narrowed arteries may be unable to deliver enough blood and oxygen to the brain. When the brain does not receive the blood it needs, a stroke occurs. A stroke can occur if an artery in the brain is weakened and the pressure causes it to burst.

Diabetes increases the potential for circulatory problems, which can lead to a higher incidence of stroke.

The risk factors are very similar for many diseases that occur with aging. Some of the risk factors that can't be changed are age, sex, race, and family history of stroke.

Review again the risk factors: obesity, high blood pressure, high cholesterol, heart disease, circulatory problems such as diabetes, lack of exercise, drinking alcohol in excess, and smoking. Many of these lifestyle factors are in your control and can be modified, eliminated, and changed.

These last five Keys were not intended to alarm or depress you. But, if all of us make an effort to learn more about these conditions, the quality and quantity of our lives could be enhanced. It is a privilege, not a punishment, to grow old, but we must take the good news along with the bad news. A positive attitude toward all of life will cause much less pain and suffering even in the midst of these afflictions.

44
FOOD SENSITIVITIES AND ALLERGIES

One of the most common but not life threatening problems that can occur at any stage of life is a sensitivity to foods or perhaps an allergy. There is a fine line between a food sensitivity and an allergy. Usually when you eat something to which you are allergic, your body reacts immediately and there are symptoms such as sneezing, sinus congestion, swelling of the throat, inability to breathe, nausea, a rash, or hives.

More people are sensitive, rather than allergic to a food. If you are sensitive to a food, your body may not react for several hours or even until the following day. Some of these symptoms can be chronic sinus congestion, headaches, diarrhea, lack of energy, irritability, mood swings, and reduced mental clarity. Other symptoms, such as aching joints and muscles, can be associated with food sensitivities.

It is impossible to diagnose food intolerance without proper medical exams by an allergist. Allergies and sensitivities can be related to genetics and hereditary factors. New clinical studies show that some lifestyle factors can contribute to food sensitivities. Many times food allergies and sensitivities develop in childhood and are outgrown in maturity. The opposite also can be true, however, and the older we get, the more severe a reaction can be to a specific food. Our immune system could be at fault. The ability to fight off the negative effects can be manifested in more extreme symptoms.

One problem that seems to increase as we age is the inability to digest milk products. *Lactose intolerance* is the inability of the small intestine to break down milk sugar (lactose) into its constituent simple sugars (glucose and lactose) because the body doesn't manufacture enough of the necessary enzyme, lactase. The symptoms of lactose intolerance include gas, bloating, abdominal pain, diarrhea, and a rumbling stomach. A physician can rule out other causes of these symptoms. There is no cure, but it can be controlled.

The natural foods with lactose are dairy products, but it is important to read labels as there are many other foods that contain lactose. People have lactose intolerance in varying degrees. Many still can digest lactose in small quantities. Some dairy products are naturally low in lactose, such as yogurt, buttermilk, and cheeses. All of these are cultured or fermented and in the process some of the lactase is broken down.

If dairy products do need to be eliminated from the diet, it will be necessary to find other sources of calcium. You might want to consult a registered dietitian to find ways of adding more calcium to the diet.

There are now lactose-reduced dairy products available at most dairy counters, such as sweet acidophilus milk or lactaid milk. They usually are well marked. A lactase enzyme tablet also is available. It can be added to foods containing dairy products or tablets that can be taken orally. Read the directions carefully for any of these products. These can decrease the symptoms of lactose intolerance in some people.

Anyone could be allergic to certain foods in any food group. If you have some of the unexplained symptoms mentioned above, be aware of the foods you eat and consider seeking guidance from an allergist. A food/drink and medication diary is a tool to discovering a sensitivity. Along with your food intake, record physical and emotional feelings and you may begin to see a correlation. With some creative planning, you still can enjoy good quality foods even if you might be sensitive or allergic to others.

45

DRUG AND FOOD
INTERACTIONS

The Food and Drug Administration has done an admirable job of regulating prescription and over-the-counter (OTC) drugs for us. They also have announced that soon drug companies will be required to provide information to doctors regarding the unique effects prescription drugs have on older people. However we laymen must take more responsibility for educating ourselves on the difficult and complex problem of accurately determining the effect of food and nutrients on a particular drug. Communication is the key word. We must read the written word on drugs and understand the interactions and consequences. It is imperative to ask your health care provider, pharmacist, or registered dietitian about drug/nutrient interactions.

The interaction between foods and drugs, and drugs and other drugs, depends on a variety of factors. Some of these are the drug dosage and the individual's age, size, and specific medical condition. Some foods can affect the way drugs behave in the body.

One of the greatest concerns with older individuals is polypharmacy, which is the use of several drugs (generally three or more). As was pointed out in the preceding Keys, the incidence of many mild and serious health problems multiplies with age. Older people take more drugs than younger individuals do.

There is a close interrelationship between nutrients and drugs. The percentage of lean body mass decreases, whereas the percentage of fat tissue increases. The percentage of water also decreases. These changes can affect the amount of drug absorption, the minimum safe dosage, and the length of time a drug stays in the body.

With age, the kidneys and liver function less efficiently. They are responsible for breaking down and removing most drugs from the body. Undesirable reactions can occur because drugs leave the body more slowly. Another problem is that the decreased amount of gastric acid can lead to acidic drugs being poorly absorbed. A major way foods affect drugs is by enhancing or impeding the rate at which the drugs enter the bloodstream.

Each person is unique. Some individuals can take many drugs without side effects, whereas others have negative reactions ranging from mild to severe.

What can you do to take more responsibility for the prescription drugs and medications you take? Ask your physician and pharmacist questions: What is the medication for? When is this to be taken? How often should I take this? Should I take it with food or on an empty stomach? Should I take it with water or some other liquid? How should I store the medicine? Can I take it along with other medications or prescriptions? How long should I continue to take it? When do I need to check with the doctor again? Are there foods and beverages I should avoid? What about side effects of alcohol? Can I drive a car after I take this medication? What adverse consequences should I be on the lookout for? You can add individual questions to this list, depending on your health history and your particular illness or disease. Don't be hesitant to ask your doctor any questions you may have concerning your medications.

You should make a commitment to read all labels and brochures that accompany a drug or medicine. In order for a drug to retain its potency, the method of storage is important. Some drugs are sensitive to sunlight and heat, or may need to be stored at a cool temperature.

Keep a detailed record of every drug you take and carry the list with you at all times. Have your doctor evaluate your medications. Bring all your prescriptions, over-the-counter medicine, and nutritional supplements on the next visit to your doctor. He should take the time to explain everything to you.

Learn to read the label on the bottle. Request that the pharmacist print the label in large letters, so it is easily readable. The information on the label includes the name of the drug, the dosage, the form (capsule, tablet, liquid), the strength, the number you will get, directions for use, and the amount of times a prescription can be refilled.

Each drug and medication can have distinct side effects and affect each individual differently. Be sure to have your health care professional write down the side effects for each drug you are taking. Dispose of old drugs by flushing them down the toilet. Never take medications prescribed for anyone else. Never stop your medication unless you have discussed the change with your doctor. Do not stop taking a drug simply because it is too expensive. Your doctor or social service can help you find a way to buy the medication less expensively. If you have more than one doctor, make sure each one knows what the other is giving you.

With the number of over-the-counter drugs on the increase, treat these medications just as significantly as your prescription drugs. Follow the same rules and ask the same questions.

The growth of the generic drug industry is sizable. Generics are less costly and are scrutinized by the Food and Drug Administration just as carefully as the regular drugs and medicines. Be cautious and ask the pharmacist or your physician if there is a generic form before you fill the prescription. Ask about quality control of the generic brand. Remember, your reactions to a drug at ages thirty, fifty, and eighty can be entirely different.

This is a very important Key. Do not overuse or abuse any type of drug or medication. Learn more about your specific health problems, sensitivities, the drugs you are using, and their side effects.

46

ALCOHOL/SUBSTANCE ABUSE

Some people might ask, "Why include a chapter on alcohol and substance abuse in a book on nutrition for the over fifty population?" Isn't this a problem of the young? This is an inaccuracy that needs to be dispelled. Alcoholism is a major health problem crossing all age groups. The aging population might be known to drink less as a group, but the problem of drinking by older people is an enormous dilemma, and is predicted to grow appreciably in the next several years.

Many individuals, at one time or another in their lives, could have abused alcohol or drugs. *Abuse* is the improper use of something, the practice of mistreating or misusing a substance. *Dependency* and *addiction* are the need to rely on alcohol and drugs for aid and support. Authorities in the field of addictions believe that alcohol is the most serious drug problem facing older persons.

Problem drinking is defined as anyone who drinks enough for it to interfere with physical and social functioning. Older adults who abuse alcohol are classified into two groups—the ones who have been drinking excessively for most of their lives and the ones who started at a later age. The problem is complex and there are various degrees of concern and danger. Some of the reasons for alcohol abuse in older individuals include insomnia, the need to numb pain, the loss of self-esteem, the death of loved ones, a feeling of uselessness upon retirement and the end of child rearing, boredom, more discretionary income and leisure time, stress from health and financial worries, and alienation from family and friends.

Alcohol use and the aging process are incompatible. Tolerance for alcohol generally decreases with age, so one usually cannot consume the same amount as someone younger. The older person will be more affected for a longer period of time. Signs of alcohol abuse can imitate other disorders, such as depression, memory loss, and insomnia. Alcohol also can conceal other illnesses because it can disguise pain.

Alcoholism is an illness that can seriously impact other illnesses and diseases. Alcohol travels in the bloodstream to all organs, and can exacerbate ailments of the liver, pancreas, intestines, circulatory system, and nervous system. It affects the heart, blood pressure, and diabetes. It decreases heart efficiency and diminishes the flow of oxygen to the brain. Another significant problem is the interaction of alcohol with other drugs. Prescription and over-the-counter drugs may not mix favorably with alcohol. People who take one or several medications are at risk of adverse side effects. Alcohol can interfere with heart and blood pressure medication, and also with tranquilizers, barbiturates, painkillers, and antihistamines. Some drugs are metabolized more rapidly with the concurrent use of alcohol, such as antidiabetes drugs, anticoagulants, and anticonvulsants.

It is also very possible to become addicted to some of the prescription drugs. Be aware and informed about the drugs being consumed. Communication with your doctor is important. If there is any doubt about negative side effects of drinking and taking any medication, *do not drink!*

Some of the warning signs that indicate a possible alcohol problem include having an unexplained accident or fall; getting drunk often; loss of interest in family, friends, and activities; gulping drinks; drinking alone; preferring a drink over a meal; needing to drink daily and in increasing amounts; mood swings; short-term memory loss; and lack of interest in personal appearance and in the cleanliness of the home. These are some of the signals that indicate a problem!

What are the biggest consequences of alcohol as related to nutrition? A problem drinker often experiences a loss of appetite. Signs of malnutrition appear because alcohol is being substituted for other nutrients. Alcohol contains empty calories, which are deficient in nutrients. Frequently, alcohol replaces food intake.

There is no other illness where the denial of a problem is so strong as in alcohol and drug abuse. It not only affects the individual with the problem but also the family, friends, and everyone in that person's circle. It has negative consequences on physical, mental, emotional, and spiritual health.

If help is sought and employed, the chances for recovery from substance abuse are very good, although there is no permanent cure. To seek assistance and obtain more information, write the National Clearinghouse for Alcohol and Drug Information (NCADI), P.O. Box 2345, Dept. ELDY, Rockville, Maryland 20852. This is a federal information service that answers public inquiries and distributes written material. The National Council on Alcoholism (NCA) can refer you to treatment services in your area and distributes literature. Write NCA, 733 Third Avenue, New York, New York 10017. Alcoholics Anonymous (AA) is a voluntary worldwide fellowship. Its purpose is to help oneself and others stay sober. For information, write to the national office at P.O. Box 459, Grand Central Station, New York, New York 10163, or phone your local chapter.

It is much easier to ignore an issue such as alcoholism and drug abuse. But, pretending the situation does not exist only will do a disservice to the person who has the problem and everyone else. By addressing this issue, you can be giving yourself or someone you love a new lease on life.

47

ADDITIVES/CHEMICAL CONTAMINATION

Most of us did not grow up hearing such words as additives, preservatives, and pesticides. When we hear those words and others like them today, we shudder because of their negative impact. The question is whether there is anything that is safe to eat! This is currently a controversial area of nutrition, and conflicting reports are circulated causing concern for consumers. The best procedure to follow is to survey the facts, evaluate them, get some professional advice, and then do what is comfortable and not worrisome.

Science and technology have come a long way for the benefit of consumers. Authorities believe that microbiological contamination of food (see Key 30) is a much greater threat than the additive and pesticide scare. The manner in which food is handled, stored, and prepared is the main factor in preventing food contamination.

Additives are substances added to food for a purpose. They preserve and increase the shelf life of products, slow or prevent microbe growth, enhance the nutritional value, improve taste, texture, appeal, and appearance, and replace nutrients that were removed in the refining process. If it weren't for additives, bread would mold, marshmallows would be hard, and ice cream would have ice crystals. Attractive taste, texture, color, and appeal of foods would be lessened. Food could not be stored for any length of time. Grocery shopping would have to be done every day.

The Food and Drug Administration regulates the control and safety of chemicals added to foods. *Safety* is defined as a reasonable certainty that no harm will result from the use of an additive.

Let's look at some of the food additives and how they are used. The names read like a chemistry textbook. It is not necessary to learn them, but become familiar with their applications.

Antioxidants are used to prevent oxidation, which results in rancidity of fats or browning of fruits. Other preservatives are used to control the growth of bacteria, yeast, and mold. They are used in such foods as vegetable shortenings, oils, pudding and pie filling mixes, canned and frozen fruit, bread, cheese, fruit juices, and sodas.

Nutrient supplements are mainly vitamins and minerals added to improve the nutrient value of foods, such as vitamin A-, C-, and D-fortified milk, margarine, iodized salt, fortified breakfast cereals, and enriched rice and flour.

Emulsifiers make it possible to disperse particles that normally do not mix together, such as oil and water. Consistency and texture are improved. Stabilizers and thickeners aid in maintaining smooth texture and uniform color and flavor. They are added to pudding mixes, ice creams, cream cheese, baked goods, jams, jellies, candies, and sauces.

Bases and acids control the alkalinity and acidity of many food products and create a medium unfavorable to microbe growth.

Artificial sweeteners are used as a substitute for sugar. *Artificial colorings* are used in margarine, cheese, jams and jellies, fruit-flavored gelatins, pudding and pie filling mixes. *Flavoring and flavoring agents* are added to foods to give a more pronounced taste. This list could be even further expanded! So beware, "What you see, is what you get" is not necessarily so! Be a conscientious reader of labels. As new research is implemented, improvements will be made. For example, sulfites are now being banned on fresh potatoes. This is the substance that prevents spoilage and discoloration of fresh vegetables and fruits in restaurant salad bars. This is no longer legal. Many people are allergic to sulfites and must

144

avoid them. Nitrates are used in canned foods to prevent botulism.

The use of pesticides is another topic that raises numerous queries from consumers. *Pesticides* are chemicals applied in the production and storage of raw agricultural commodities. Residues may remain on the marketable food. All of the agricultural chemicals (pesticides, fungicides, insecticides) have specific purposes. Scientists constantly are striving to increase the amount of safe chemicals to be used. The aim is to ensure the safety of crop and water supplies.

When I look back at the type of farming my father did, it was all organic. So another "new" word really is an "old" word. Organic farming is a gigantic industry. It is a production system that avoids the use of synthetic fertilizer, pesticides, livestock feed additives, and growth regulators. To us, the consumer, organic food signifies food that is raised without any chemicals involved, including any artificial fertilizers, pesticides, fungicides, or herbicides. The food is not treated or enhanced with artificial preservatives or additives. It sounds wonderful in theory, but at this stage of technology is it practical and is it going to happen? These are very debatable questions.

On the practical and personal side, be sure to wash and scrub fresh fruit and vegetables thoroughly with tepid water. Produce can be peeled, but that reduces the intake of fiber, so this can be a trade-off! Remove the outer leaves of lettuce and cabbage.

Yes, there is anxiety concerning cancer and other illnesses, but the risks must be weighed against the benefits. It is more important to have a diet that includes a variety of high value nutrient-dense foods, eaten in moderation and enjoyment, than to live with excess fear and eliminate any of the food groups.

48

VEGETARIAN COOKING AND EATING

Vegetarianism is not a new wave concept, but goes back to the Stone Age and the ancient scriptures. It seems to fluctuate in popularity. Today it is very much in vogue, due to the current emphasis on low-fat, low-cholesterol, and high fiber eating.

There are several classifications of vegetarianism. A strict vegetarian diet, called a *vegan diet*, excludes all meat, eggs, and dairy products. A *lacto-vegetarian diet* includes milk products; a *lacto-ovo-vegetarian diet* includes eggs and dairy products; and a *pesco-vegetarian diet* includes fish and seafood. There are many reasons why people choose one of these types of diets, among them health concerns, moral, ethical, or social responsibilities, and environmental and global implications. In this Key, we are concerned primarily with health reasons.

What are some health concerns that could affect our decision to try alternative eating? It has been established that vegetarians usually have lower levels of cholesterol, a decreased risk of hardening of the arteries and heart attacks, a lesser degree of some types of cancer, and fewer reports of bacterial diseases such as salmonellosis and trichinosis. Vegetarians also claim that allergies disappear, food craving is limited, weight is under control, disposition is less harried, and there is an overall feeling of improved health and a sense of well-being. Added benefits seem to be increased energy and endurance and a savings in the food budget.

Instead of concentrating on what we would have to give up in our diet, think about the food that is allowed. The same four food groups are used in the most common vegetarian diet, the lacto-ovo-vegetarian. The only change is in the meat groups where legumes are selected, such as peanut butter, peas, dried beans, and nuts. These groups provide all the complex carbohydrates, proteins, fat, and vitamins and minerals necessary to sustain health.

The question that always arises is what about protein? *Amino acids* are the building blocks of protein. There are eight essential amino acids, meaning they cannot be produced by the body and must be obtained from the diet (the nonessential amino acids are produced in our body by modifying other protein). Meat is a complete protein; it contains all eight of the essential amino acids we need for cell renewal and repair. The challenge is to get a complete protein from the vegetable based diet. This is done by combining an incomplete protein with another food that complements it or completes the need for all the amino acids. Any legume and grain combination makes a complete protein. An example is a peanut butter sandwich: the peanut butter is the legume and the wheat bread is the grain.

Many countries have staple foods that naturally provide a complete protein—the bean burrito of Mexico, beans and rice from Japan, hummus (ground garbanzo beans) and pita bread in the Far East.

A vegetable with a grain or legume also works. Grains served with a small amount of cheese or milk also greatly enhance the quality of protein from the grains. The classic examples are cereal with milk or a cheese sandwich. Additionally, complementary foods don't need to be consumed at the same meal, just during the same day. The addition of eggs to a vegetarian diet is helpful because the protein found in the egg white is of very high quality. The essential amino acids are present in ratios closely matched to the human need.

If the diet restricts dairy foods, the issue of calcium intake must be considered. Besides milk and cheese, the major food sources of calcium are turnip and mustard greens, collards, kale, and broccoli. These vegetables also provide iron. The need for calcium may be even less for vegetarians, because a diet excessive in protein (typical to a meat based diet) inter-

147

feres with calcium absorption. On the other hand, there are compounds called oxylates and phylates found in vegetables and grains that bind with calcium and prevent it from being absorbed. A strict vegetarian should consider a calcium supplement.

When considering a nonmeat diet, do not overlook nuts and seeds. They contain protein, vitamins and minerals, and also fat. The fat is largely unsaturated, but it still is fat, so limit your intake to no more than one tablespoon per day. Although they add variety, texture, and flavor to dishes, use nuts and seeds with discretion.

Another staple in a vegetarian diet is legumes. *Legumes* are the seeds of plants that bear pods. The legume itself has two halves like a peanut. It is a broad family that includes beans, peas, peanuts, and lentils. More than half the world lives on this kind of diet. A cookbook I have lists 20 distinct varieties in this grouping, and many, many recipes to go with each type. They are used in soups, as spreads or dips, as main dishes, combined with meat and other vegetables, as a salad, and as desserts. They contain dietary fiber, protein, and abundant vitamins and minerals.

Soybeans are also in the legume family. One interesting form of soybeans is tofu. *Tofu* is the curd or cheese of soybeans that has been pressed into solid squares. It actually does provide a complete protein but a few of the essential amino acids are quite low, so it still should be complemented with a grain or vegetable. It is low in cost. Tofu is packed in water and should be stored that way, changing the water daily. It is wonderful in soups, main dishes, and as a substitute for cheese. Tofu takes on the flavor of other foods and sauces it is mixed with.

A Key unto themselves are health foods, natural foods, and organically-grown products. We should be aware of what is happening in this area. Many health foods are not really any "healthier" than regular foods purchased, so it is imperative to check out any claims made of them. The term "natural," as related to foods, is a general term that can have so many meanings it is virtually too broad to define. For instance, many candy bars sold at health food stores are indeed made of natural ingredients, but they still are high in sugar and fat. The best advice is to investigate, be educated, and ask questions.

Should a vegetarian diet be considered? My recommendation is to give vegetarian cooking and eating a try, not necessarily a complete switch over to a vegetarian diet but perhaps several meals a week or a couple of days a week. Before you cut out meat, you need to be competent at combining incomplete protein foods to make them complete. Many restaurants offer this type of selection on their menus. If you are insecure about getting the adequate foods for complete nutrition, there are many cookbooks and classes to help you plan effectively. You would not have to change completely, but it could be regarded as an alternative.

49

FOOD FACTS AND FADS

According to the National Council Against Health Fraud, a quack is "anyone who promotes health remedies and schemes known to be unsafe, unproven, or false, for financial gain." When individuals are *so* desperate to regain optimum health they are willing to try anything. By delaying proper medical treatment, there can be deplorable results. The common areas in which deceit is rampant are aging, weight loss, arthritis, and cancer.

Health quackery is a billion dollar industry. Everyone wants to improve the quality of his or her life and many times it is difficult to distinguish between a fact and a fad. Many food products and supplements, medicines, and medical devices are misrepresented, mislabeled, and sometimes harmful. The first place to start is with your doctor. Ask questions, then do some investigating on your own.

Some people are always searching for the "fountain of youth." Products that claim to stop or reverse the aging process and cure arthritis and cancer are common. Cosmetics companies that claim to erase wrinkles, firm and tone your body, give you extra energy, and enhance virility are just some of the deceptions. Is there an effortless way to lose weight? You would think so by the advertising of no diet and no exercise, but consequent weight loss of ten pounds a week that appears in all the media. Millions of people buy and use these pills and products weekly. They are expensive and potentially dangerous.

The quacks have jumped on the bandwagon and offer remedies for every type of arthritis imaginable. Medical science has found effective treatments for arthritis, but there is no cure. Symptoms many times will subside, and if someone is on an unethical treatment, he or she may believe that this actually is what helped. Some clinics outside the United States use untested diets and drugs, often resulting in additional health problems.

One of the most tragic situations is advertised cures for cancer. Individuals who are seriously ill and grasping at straws are willing to try anything. Many of these cures claim to treat all kinds of cancer, but have no proven value and can be life threatening. Due to medically proven technology, the survival rate of individuals with cancer is expanding rapidly. The cancer must be detected and treated quickly, and precious time is wasted by trying unethical therapy and treatments.

What can we consumers do to prevent these companies from taking advantage of us? Watch for false advertising that promises special, secret, quick, painless cures, outrageous claims, testimonials, or one product that cures a multitude of ailments. Sometimes products claim to be so new, modern technology hasn't caught on to them yet. They may claim that the medical society purposely ignores the therapy in order to preserve these lucrative technologies. Beware of health fraud sent through the mail. It may seem so promising and relatively inexpensive. Health fraud is a multibillion dollar industry and it is estimated that as much as 60 percent of the dollars spent on health fraud products comes out of the pockets of older adults. Use a common sense approach along with "buyer beware" thinking. Do some investigating and check with the Better Business Bureau, State Consumer Affairs Office, Food and Drug Administration, Federal Trade Commission, and Postal Inspection Service.

We are bombarded with new science and research making it extremely difficult to distinguish a food fact from a food fad. Can you believe the labels? Trust is a wonderful attribute, but I challenge you to read carefully and do not be afraid to ask a lot of questions.

50

50 TIPS TO FITNESS OVER FIFTY

Here are 50 tips to get you started on a new outlook on life. They are listed in categories: physical, mental, emotional, spiritual, nutritional, and miscellaneous suggestions.

- Balance physical, mental, emotional, and spiritual health.
- Strengthen your muscles.
- Improve your posture.
- Breathe correctly and deeply.
- Exercise regularly.
- Read *Keys to Fitness Over Fifty*.
- Get the "More Alive" exercise video.
- Try a new sport.
- Do flexibility exercises.
- Do an aerobic exercise.
- Stay active.
- Develop a new hobby.
- Read a book for fun.
- Take a class.
- Be a community volunteer.
- Have a positive attitude.
- Plan ahead/keep a journal.
- Be happy.
- Smile and laugh more.
- Love and hug more.
- Learn to relax.
- Make new friends.
- Control your stress.
- Worry less.
- Count your blessings.
- Be patient with yourself and others.
- Meditate/pray.

- Relish quietness.
- Phone a lonely person.
- Do a good deed daily.
- Eat a variety of foods.
- Increase calcium in your diet.
- Maintain a desirable weight.
- Eat more fruits, vegetables, and grain products.
- Eat a balanced diet.
- Lower your consumption of fat.
- Drink more water.
- Use salt in moderation.
- Plan nutritious menus.
- Cut down on food portion sizes.
- If you drink alcohol, do so in moderation.
- Follow all of the suggestions in this book.
- Don't smoke.
- Have regular health checkups.
- Check safety in your home.
- Wear a sunscreen.
- If problems arise, consult a doctor.
- Get adequate rest.
- Use your seat belt.
- Add 50 more tips to this list!

SUMMARY

We packed a lot of information in 50 keys, but a suitable summary is the same as the one in my book, *Keys to Fitness Over Fifty*. The theme song, "We've Only Just Begun," certainly is true of nutrition as well as fitness over fifty.

Research, studies, and statistics in the field of nutrition are very confusing and contradictory, especially pertaining to the over fifty age group. There have been too few participants in the studies. The studies have not been done for a long enough time period, and some of the experiments have been done only on animals. Additional information appears almost daily, so check it out, do some research yourself, take a class, and ask your doctor and dietitian for their opinions. It is important to keep abreast of the constantly changing world of nutrition.

I hope this book has heightened your awareness of many things that you already knew, enlivened your shopping experience, led you to examine your kitchen, and provided fresh insights on cooking, eating, and nutrition. Use this book as a reference tool, a helpful guide as you continue to learn, grow, and obtain new beneficial knowledge.

The key is to improve your lifestyle in all areas, use common sense, do everything in moderation, and by all means, *enjoy life!*

So, remember, every day in every way you can feel good, better, and even best, by living the "More Alive" way. The key is "We've Only Just Begun."

I sincerely want you to enjoy healthier lives. I do care about each and every one of you, and wish you peace, love, and joy! God bless.

Yours, for better aging,
Jo Murphy

Note: The "More Alive" exercises are available on a 60-minute video or audio cassette tape. For *Nutrition Over Fifty* and *Fitness Over Fifty* readers, the video is $19.95 plus $3.00 for shipping and handling (also available captioned for the hearing impaired). The audio cassette is $9.95 plus $3.00. The video consists of seven nonaerobic segments to stretch, tone, and strengthen every area of the body. It's safe, fun, and effective increasing flexibility, strength, and endurance. The exercises are adaptable to all fitness levels. Each exercise is demonstrated in detail and you gradually can increase the repetitions.

If you use this video on a regular schedule, you will look and feel better. By purchasing this video, you have made a decision to improve the quality of your life. To order, send a check or money order to Mature Adult Corporation, P.O. Box 31872, Aurora, CO 80041

QUESTIONS AND ANSWERS

Q. Which calcium supplement should I take?

A. Calcium carbonate, also known as oyster shell, is the least expensive and contains the highest amount of elemental calcium per tablet. However, if you lack stomach acids, calcium citrate is easiest to digest. Calcium lactate and gluconate have relatively low amounts of calcium. Bonemeal and dolomite are not recommended due to possible contamination by poisonous metals.

Q. How do I know if I should take a supplement?

A. Without the help of a dietitian, you will need to analyze your diet yourself. Keep a food diary for two or three days. Do you average 2 meat, 2–3 milk, 2–5 fruit and vegetable, and 6–11 bread/grain servings each day? If not, try to improve your diet to satisfy the four food groups plan. If this is not possible, you may benefit from a multivitamin/mineral supplement. Never purchase one that provides greater than 100 percent of the USRDA of each vitamin and mineral. Remember it is a *supplement* to your diet, not a replacement for food. Take it every other day or once a day with a meal.

Q. I feel I don't digest food as well as I used to. It seems the food sits in my stomach for hours. Is there anything I can do?

A. Yes. First, you may learn that there are some foods you simply need to avoid. Chew your food thoroughly so your digestive system has less work to do. There are numerous digestive enzyme supplements available in health food and grocery stores that may help. Some are quite simple, containing only papain or bromelain (natural digestive enzymes from papaya and pineapple), others contain a variety of digestive enzymes. Never take these over-the-counter digestive aids without consulting your health care provider first.

Q. Can I lose weight simply by cutting down on food?

A. Yes and no. That's a good start. More specifically, you should focus on cutting down on high-fat and empty calorie foods. Moreover, weight loss by diet alone is difficult, especially as you get older. Exercise is a crucial element in any weight loss plan and makes the process a lot more enjoyable.

Q. Over the years, I have gained a few pounds and I just can't get back to the weight I was when I married. What should I do?

A. Relax; studies indicate that the healthy weight range for older persons includes 20–30 pounds more than when they were in their twenties. Some weight gain with age is expected, normal, and healthy.

Q. All the information on fat and cholesterol is confusing me. What are the most effective things I can do to watch the amount of fat in my diet?

A. Read labels, choose products with less than 2–3 grams of fat per serving, don't fry food, and use sparingly butter, margarine, shortening, oil, and all products that are high in fat.

Q. Considering cholesterol and the problem with salmonella, should I avoid eggs?

A. In terms of cholesterol, the current guideline is three eggs a week. You can have more if you remove the egg yolk. A three-egg omelet that has only one egg yolk is an excellent source of protein, tastes fine, and is low in fat.

Salmonella food poisoning is also a worthy concern. No more runny eggs or soft-boiled eggs. The whites must be cooked until opaque and the yolk must be solid. To prevent salmonella poisoning, eggs should be washed before cracking them open and should be cooked thoroughly.

Q. I don't want to support health fraud; who can I trust for nutrition information?

A. Your doctor or registered dietitian.

Q. I have difficulties breathing after meals. Is there anything I can do?

A. Digestion requires oxygen, and shortness of breath is common after eating. Try eating six small meals a day rather than three large ones. Also, avoid large servings of concentrated sweets like ice cream, milk shakes, cake, cookies, and candy because carbohydrates require more oxygen for digestion than do protein and fats.

Q. Is it true that zinc supplementation helps improve the sense of taste and wound healing?

A. If you have a zinc deficiency, a zinc supplement may restore taste and improve wound healing. If you do not have a deficiency, supplementation is useless. This is another area where you must seek the advice of your health care professional before experimenting with any supplements.

Q. Should I take a vitamin C supplement?

A. Fewer than 10 milligrams of vitamin C is needed to prevent scurvy. The RDA is 60 milligrams per day, and 100 milligrams per day will completely saturate your tissues. Vitamin C is water soluble and cannot be stored very well, so excesses are lost through the urine. During times of stress, your supply of vitamin C is depleted because it is involved in the release of stress hormones epinephrine and norepinephrine. During these times, extra servings of vitamin C rich foods may be helpful. If you take a supplement, buy one with the lowest amount possible, usually about 250 milligrams.

INFORMATION GUIDE

American Cancer Society
  70 East Lake Street, Suite 600
  Chicago, IL 60601

American Diabetes Association
  1660 Duke Street
  Alexandria, VA 22314

American Diabetic Association
  216 West Jackson Boulevard, Suite 800
  Chicago, IL 60606

American Heart Association
  National Center
  7320 Greenville Avenue
  Dallas, TX 75231

Arthritis Foundation
  1314 Spring Street, N.W.
  Atlanta, GA 30309

National Dairy Council
  6300 North River Road
  Rosemont, IL 60018-4233

National Osteoporosis Foundation
  1625 Eye Street, N.W.
  Washington, DC 20006

National Stroke Association
  3001 East Hampton Avenue, Suite 240
  Englewood, CO 80110-2622

GLOSSARY

Amino acid the units from which protein is synthesized and into which it is broken down during digestion.

Calorie a unit of energy that may be obtained from food.

Carbohydrate a food composed of carbon and hydrogen that provides four calories of energy per gram.

Cholesterol a fatty waxy-like substance found in the diet from animal products and also produced in the body.

Complementary proteins the foods that combine with each other to provide all eight essential amino acids.

Complex carbohydrates the foods made up of many simple monosaccharide units, such as starch and cellulose; found in cereals, potatoes, and legumes.

Diverticuli the pouches or pockets found in the intestine caused by abdominal pressure associated with constipation.

Dysphagia a condition of difficulty in swallowing.

Empty calories a food that is low in vitamins, minerals, and fiber, but provides calories.

Essential amino acids the organic compounds that cannot be manufactured within the body and must be provided in the diet.

Food allergy an adverse reaction to a food for which an immunological pathogen can be demonstrated.

Food intolerance a general term for an abnormal physiological response to a food where the mechanism is unknown or nonimmunologic.

Hypertension a condition of high blood pressure.

Insoluble fiber the part of a plant that gives it structure, and helps sweep the bowels clean.

Low calorie a label that indicates less than 40 calories per serving.

161

Low cholesterol diet a diet of less than 300 milligrams of dietary cholesterol consumed each day.

Low-fat food a food of less than 2–3 grams of fat per serving.

Low sodium a label that indicates less than 200 milligrams per serving.

Monosaccharide a simple sugar unit.

Monounsaturated fat a fat in which one hydrogen atom is missing and is liquid at room temperature.

Nonessential amino acid an organic compound that can be synthesized by body cells as long as nitrogen is available.

Organic a term that means having its origins in living material, either plant or animal.

Osteoporosis the loss of calcium from bones resulting in weaker bones.

Perfect food a food that doesn't exist.

Polyunsaturated fat a fat that is liquid at room temperature and has very few hydrogen atoms.

Protein a compound of amino acids that is made up of carbon, hydrogen, nitrogen, and sometimes sulfur. Provides 4 calories of energy per gram.

Recommended Daily Allowances (RDA) the amount of nutrients needed to prevent a deficiency for the average person within an age group.

Registered dietitian a professional who has studied nutrition at an accredited college or university, has passed a national test on nutrition knowledge, and maintains continued education through the American Dietetic Association.

Saturated fat a fat that is heavily loaded with hydrogen atoms and is solid at room temperature, such as butter, lard, and animal fat. Additionally, coconut and palm oil are saturated.

Soluble fiber the gum, pectin, and mucilage in a plant food; it does not provide calories and absorbs large quantities of water.

Unit pricing the labels that tell how much a food costs per unit (ounce, pound) and are posted on the shelf edge directly below or above items in the grocery.

INDEX